BARE
ESSENTIALS

UNDERWEAR:
PANTIES & KNICKERS

CONSTRUCTION AND PATTERN
DRAFTING FOR LINGERIE DESIGN

PUBLICATION BY
FAIRBANKS PUBLISHING LLC
dba Porcelynne

SECOND EDITION

Jennifer Lynne Matthews - Fairbanks

Book Design by Designarchy
Cover Photography by Ashley Burke
Interior Photography by David Fairbanks
Written by Jennifer Lynne Matthews-Fairbanks

Universities and wholesale purchasing:

Fairbanks Publishing offers special rates for universities and wholesale purchasing.

Wholesale purchasing is available through Ingram Distribution or directly through Porcelynne.com.

Updates:

Information contained in this book was current at the time of publishing. For updates, check our blog: https://blog.porcelynne.com.

Contact Us:

Fairbanks Publishing LLC, dba Porcelynne at info@porcelynne.com.

Your feedback is always welcome. Let us know if we can do anything to improve this title.

First Edition B&W: ISBN-10: 0983132828, ISBN-13: 978-0-9831328-2-0
Second Edition B&W: ISBN: 979-8-7259833-1-9
Second Edition Color: ISBN: 978-1-7332740-8-1

CONTENTS

CONTENTS

INTERMEDIATE

ADVANCED

PATTERNS

CHAPTER 21

PREFACE

As a lingerie designer and educator, I felt there was a gap in educational texts for lingerie design. I compiled this information for educational purposes, from personal experience and experimentation. The book series is designed to take an individual from the process of sewing lingerie, to making pattern modifications and drafting from measurements.

This book covers many different aspects of the design process and is divided into three basic sections. As one progresses through the book, the directions become more complex, allowing each individual to master the art of lingerie design through construction, pattern manipulation and pattern drafting.

Each step in the book has been tested by both students and educators to achieve the best information possible. The second edition covers manipulations with a sloper, rather than modifying basic patterns. This edition also covers how to alter a pattern for fit based on body structure.

Enjoy your venture into designing and creating your own lingerie.

- Jennifer Matthews-Fairbanks

Jennifer Lynne Matthews-Fairbanks was an instructor at the Fashion Institute of Design and Merchandising in Los Angeles and San Francisco for nine years. She owned and operated her own lingerie design business, Porcelynne Lingerie, for 10+ years and has been working as a freelance pattern maker for nearly 20 years.

A special thanks to my husband, David Fairbanks, for being there for me every step of the way, and to my beautiful daughter Emily, for being the unstoppable force of a stubborn duplicate of myself.

BEGINNER

CHAPTER 1

INTRODUCTION TO LINGERIE CONSTRUCTION

A basic understanding of garment construction is required prior to beginning a journey into lingerie design. The beginner section of this book introduces basic panty construction and working with stretch fabrics. For the sake of understanding terminologies, the terms underwear, panties, and knickers are used interchangeably. In the United States, panties are called underwear. In an effort to ease confusion, the term underwear is used exclusively for the cover text.

TOOLS & SUPPLIES

For seasoned sewers, many of these tools may already be present in sewing kits. For those just starting out in the field of sewing, this is a suggested shopping list.

Dressmaker Pins – There are a variety of different pins available for sewing. Some are very pliable and made from less than quality materials, while others are sturdy and strong. Each type of pin has a specific purpose. Be sure to get pins that are appropriate for the project. Silk pins are recommended for more delicate fabrics.

Alternatively, many sewers utilize clips instead of pins entirely. Wonder Clips™ are a popular brand for the task at hand.

Fabric Shears and Scissors – The words shears and scissors can be interchanged, although shears is the industry standard term. Be sure to keep a pair of quality shears designated for fabric use only.

Paper Scissors – A pair of scissors specifically used for cutting paper products is also necessary.

Pattern Paper – Pattern or dot paper is used in the industry for drafting. The markings may not be dots, but may contain numbers and letters on a grid. This type of paper is referred to as alpha-numeric paper. Pattern paper may not be available in all areas. Poster paper, craft paper or tracing paper can be used as acceptable alternatives.

Pattern Weights – Pattern weights can be in the form of small bean bags or as bars of steel. They are versatile and are used to stabilize a pattern, whether tracing a pattern piece or using it to hold down fabric.

Pencils – In order to get accurate shapes and edges, a mechanical pencil or a pencil with a very sharp point is necessary. A few colored pencils are handy to help differentiate pattern line changes.

Rotary Cutters and Cutting Mats – When working with small and detailed designs, using a large pair of shears is not always practical. Use of a rotary cutter or an X-Acto® knife ensures a precise cut every time.

Be sure to use a cutting mat under all work. Cutting mats come in a variety of sizes from letter size to table size. The use of rotary cutters and cutting mats is commonly used when cutting lingerie fabrics.

Straight See-Through Grid Ruler – This is important for drafting. These are generally available for both the imperial and metric systems.

For the imperial system (inches), measurements are generally taken in 8ths of an inch. The following table translates the 8ths into decimal points. This chart will prove handy when using this book in conjunction with computer aided design programs such as Adobe® Illustrator®.

The metric system (centimeters) references a millimeter (1/10), making conversions easier than the imperial system.

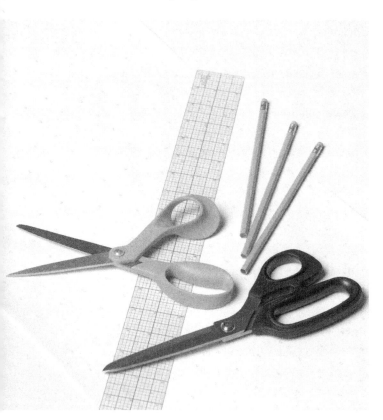

IMPERIAL MEASUREMENT CONVERSION CHART	
1/16	.06
1/8	.13
3/16	.19
1/4	.25
5/16	.31
3/8	.38
7/16	.44
1/2	.50
9/16	.56
5/8	.63
11/16	.69
3/4	.75
13/16	.81
7/8	.88
15/16	.94

Tape Measure – A soft tape measure is needed for taking measurements. Many tape measures have the imperial system on one side and the metric system on the other. Double check all tape measures against a straight ruler. Cheap tape measures may not be as accurate as one would think.

FABRIC TYPES

Fabrics generally fall into two categories: woven and knit.

Woven Fabric – Woven fabrics are comprised of threads intertwining from perpendicular directions.

Knit Fabric – These fabrics are created by a single yarn that is looped on a course. The yarn is pulled through loops to create a knit stitch on one side and a purl stitch on the other side. The knit side appears as lines of "Vs" and the purl side is compiled of loops.

FABRIC CHARACTERISTICS

Every fabric has different characteristics. Many of these characteristics can be attributed to the grainlines of the fabric.

Selvage – The selvage of a fabric is the finished edge of the fabric that runs the length of the fabric. This is found in both woven and knit fabrics.

Length Grain – This refers to the length of the fabric. This grain is parallel to the selvage and is called the warp grain in the fashion industry. It can also be referred to as the straight grain.

Knit fabrics technically do not have grainlines, but many knit fabrics have the same properties as woven fabric. The length in a knit fabric generally contains no stretch. Occasionally, the fibers knitted into a fabric may contain more stretch in the length than in the span of the fabric from selvage to selvage.

Cross Grain – When a fabric is woven the threads on the length grain are generally stationary, and weft threads are woven back and forth from edge to edge, creating the finished selvage. This weaving action causes the cross grain, or weft grain, of the fabric to have more pliability than the straight grain.

The cross "grain" of a knit usually is the stretchiest part of a knit fabric, but this is not always the case. On occasion, the length stretches more than the cross section. This is why it is important to note the direction of stretch when cutting pattern pieces out.

Bias – The bias of a fabric is the stretchiest option when using a woven fabric. Bias aligns at a 45 degree angle from the selvage. Using the bias on a knit fabric is not recommended as it does not provide additional stretch and produces unnecessary fabric waste.

Direction of Greatest Stretch (DOGS) – The term "direction of greatest stretch" or "DOGS" is used in home sewing patterns and by independent pattern designers. DOGS is not common terminology in the apparel manufacturing industry. Many home sewing patterns are labeled with what appears to be a grainline (or the direction of least stretch), but is actually the DOGS. This can cause complications if the guide line on the pattern is not clearly marked as the grainline or the DOGS.

Check with the pattern directions to determine if the markings on the pattern are for grainlines or DOGS. The patterns in this book use a traditional grainline that follow the selvage on the parallel (they follow the direction of the least stretch). DOGS are generally in a direction that is horizontal on the body which allows for stretch across the body.

STRETCH FABRICS

There are many fabric options that can be used with the patterns provided in this book.

Jersey Knits – The most common knit is known as a jersey knit. This is generally found on everyday clothing such as tee shirts and panties. This fabric can contain lycra or spandex threads for additional stretch. The addition of lycra and spandex generally adds stretch to both the length and width of the fabric.

Mesh Fabrics – Mesh fabrics can be either knit or a woven, although they generally have a fair amount of stretch to them, no matter which direction is pulled. Mesh is a net-like fabric with large spaces between the yarns. This fabric oftentimes appears to be sheer.

Stretch Lace Fabric – Laces can be created with either woven or knit construction. Depending on the properties of each lace, a lace can be treated as either.

STITCHES

Lingerie can be constructed with a combination of knit and woven fabrics. Throughout this book, instructions are provided using stitches commonly found on a basic home sewing machine and serger.

KNIT FABRIC STITCHES

When sewing stretch fabrics and elastics, avoid using a straight stitch. If a stretch fabric is sewn with a straight stitch and the fabric stretches beyond the length of the stitch, the thread breaks, causing the seams to separate.

Zigzag Stitch – A zigzag stitch is a recommended stitch for sewing stretch fabrics. It allows the fabric to stretch without threads breaking.

S-Stitch or Lightning Stitch – Older machines have an s-stitch which is less common in newer machines. Newer machines tend to have a lightning stitch. This stitch appears as a straight stitch, but the stitch is created by a full stitch forward, half a stitch back, then forward a full stitch. This allows some stretch in the stitch.

Three-Step Zigzag Stitch – This is the preferred stitch when finishing lingerie. It allows for stretch and it also secures the thread in the stitch better than a traditional zigzag stitch.

Decorative Stretch Stitches – Fancy home sewing machines offer additional stitches that allow for stretching. Test each decorative stitch on a knit fabric. Test the stretch by pulling the fabric to determine if the stitches break or move with the fabric.

SPECIALTY MACHINE STITCHES

Overlock Stitch – An overlock or serger machine cuts and finishes the edge of fabric. A similar stitch, called an overcast stitch, can be sewn on a home machine, but is not necessarily suitable for stretched seams. The overlock machine generally utilizes four threads; two threads reinforce the seam and two threads form an overcast on the edge of the fabric, leaving a clean-finished edge.

Coverstitch – Coverstitch machines utilize three to four threads. A coverstitch is used in hemming garments, as well as attaching elastic around the waistline and leg openings.

This stitch is not as secure as a three step zigzag. If a coverstitch thread breaks on a garment, the entire stitch can unravel.

Merrow Stitch – A merrow stitch or a rolled hem stitch is comprised of three threads and is a finishing stitch around hems. This stitch can be created on a home serger machine and is an ideal finish to create a ruffled edge.

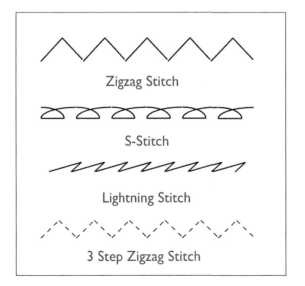

Zigzag Stitch

S-Stitch

Lightning Stitch

3 Step Zigzag Stitch

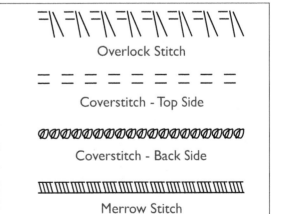

Overlock Stitch

Coverstitch - Top Side

Coverstitch - Back Side

Merrow Stitch

SPECIALTY FEET ATTACHMENTS

Binding foot – This foot can be used in attaching fold over elastic.

Roller foot – This foot is used in sewing knit fabrics. It helps roll the fabrics through the machine without stretching. It is not necessary to use such a foot, but it does make sewing knits much easier to handle under certain circumstances.

Walking foot – A walking foot can be very useful with bulky seams and stretch fabrics.

NEEDLES

Different fabrics require specific needles. Needles have a wide range in sizes, with each size used for a different purpose.

Smaller numbers indicate a finer needle and should be used for more delicate and thin fabrics. Larger numbers are a thicker needle and are used for heavier fabrics or sewing through thick layers.

Needles are generally labeled with both the American and European sizes. For example, 10/70 or 18/110. For sewing knickers and lingerie, a 10/70 or 12/80 are ideal sizes.

NEEDLE SIZES

American	European
8	60
9	65
10	70
11	75
12	80
14	90
16	100
18	110
19	120

Sharp Needles – Sharp needles are used for woven fabrics. They create straight accurate lines of stitches.

Ballpoint Needles – Ballpoint needles are used for knits. The rounder point allows the needle to safely glide between the loops of the knit without disturbing the fibers. The stitch is not as straight as with sharp needles which allows for some give on the stitch.

Universal Needles – Universal needles have many of the characteristics of both a sharp needle and a ballpoint needle. They fall in the category between sharp and ballpoint. These can be used on either wovens or knits, but if skipped stitches occur on a knit, switch the needle type to a ballpoint.

Stretch Needles – This needle is similar to a ballpoint needle but is specifically recommended when sewing Lycra®, spandex or swimwear. This needle helps to avoid skipped stitches. Some elastics require a stretch needle due to their fiber content.

Centimeters

1
2
3
4
5
6
7
8
9
10
11
12
13
14
15
16
17
18
19
20
21
22

Inches

1
2
3
4
5
6
7
8
9

BASIC PATTERNS

In the back of this book, a basic boyshort and a basic brief pattern are provided for use with this book. These patterns act as a teaching aid in understanding the basic sewing of knickers. These patterns were created from the drafting instructions in the Advanced section of this book. For sizing information, see Chapter 21.

STRETCH AND PATTERNS

Not all patterns are created equally, nor are they created for all fabrics and notions. The patterns included in this book were designed for use with a knit fabric that has about a 50% stretch in the width (cross grain) and a 35% stretch in the length. The stretch that these patterns were developed for is comparable to a jersey.

To test the stretch of a fabric, fold the fabric approximately 4" or 8 cm* away from the cut edge of the cross grain. Place two pins 5" or 10 cm* apart from each other.

Use the ruler on the left, placing one pin at the 0 mark and pull the fabric to a stretched point that meets resistance. This is not the full stretch of the fabric, but the normal stretch of the material where it hits resistance. Take a note of this amount. The ideal fabric to use with these patterns stretches on the cross grain 7.5" or 15 cm*. For fabrics that have a greater stretch in the length grain, test the stretch with the same method.

These numbers are intentionally not an equal measurement translation.

This fabric recommendation is only a suggestion based on how these patterns were developed. Use discretion in deciding on an appropriate fabric for these projects.

ELASTIC FOR BASIC PATTERNS

When sewing elastics on patterns designed with stretch, the length of elastic does not usually need to be altered.

Attaching the elastic without stretching is acceptable. When the fabric and elastic contain different stretches, alterations to the elastic may be required. Additional details on stretch are covered in the Advanced section.

Picot Edge Elastic – Picot edge elastics are available in many varieties. The picot description is of a decorative loop-type edge to an elastic. This elastic typically comes in widths of 3/8" to 5/8" (10 mm to 15 mm). The elastic itself, without the decorative edge, is usually 1/4" or 6 mm wide.

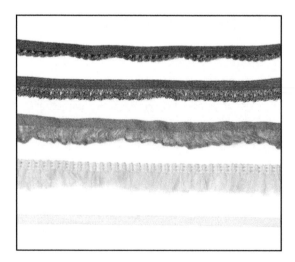

Ruffle Edge Trim – This trim is similar to the picot edge trim, but the stretch can vary from trim to trim. This trim requires careful sewing as the ruffle can easily get caught in the machine foot.

Clear Elastic – Clear elastic can be used for reinforcement on a garment to keep the integrity of a stretch lace edge or can be used to create a stretch gathered effect. For the examples in the book, this elastic is used on the edges of stretch lace trims to keep the stretch more stable. Alternatively, a stabilized tricot can be used to keep the edge from stretching.

CHAPTER 2
BASIC BOYSHORT CONSTRUCTION

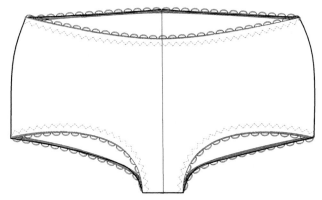

There are multiple methods to construct boyshort panties. This chapter introduces the basics. Each subsequent chapter in this section introduces alternative construction methods for further knowledge. Utilize the boyshort pattern that is provided in the back of the book. This design has a simple 3/8" to 1/2" (10mm to 12 mm) picot elastic trim applied to both the legs and waistline. In preparation, cut two fronts and two backs (mirrored), plus one lining.

1. Place the front pattern pieces together at the inner curve with the front sides facing each other. Repeat for the back pattern pieces.

Right Sides Together

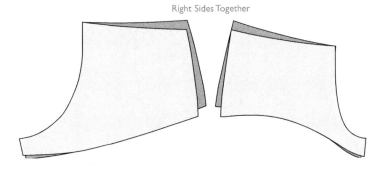

2. Stitch the curves for the fronts together using the allotted seam allowance on the patterns (1/4" or 6 mm for the provided patterns). Repeat for the back. Utilize a stretch stitch for these seams. The finished edge of the stretch stitch ends at the seam line.

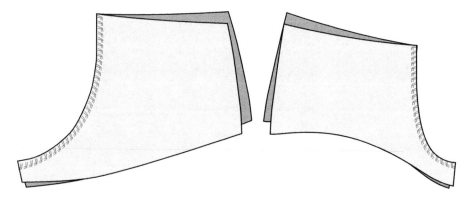

3. Open both the front and back pieces to lay flat. Line them up at the narrow edge with front sides facing each other. Stitch the lower crotch seam together with the alotted seam allowance.

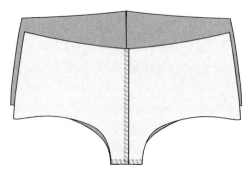

4. Finish the crotch lining edges. Overlock the short sides or fold the edges over and stitch down.

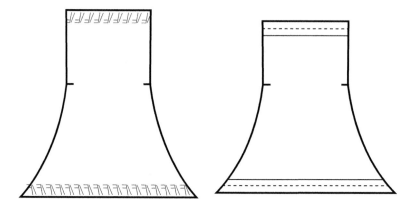

5. Open the garment flat and lay the lining over the center seam. Match the notches of the lining to the seam at the center. Stretch the lining to meet the edges of the garment and baste in place. Straight stitches are appropriate for basting these together.

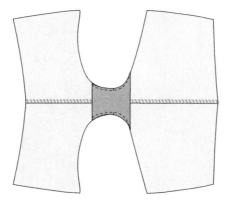

6. Place the decorative edge of the elastic towards the face side of the garment. Attach the edge of the elastic with a stretch stitch. Be sure not to stretch the fabric and be sure not to cut the elastic, if using an overlock machine. Cutting the elastic can cause the elastic to lose its stability and cause the elastic to stretch out more rapidly.

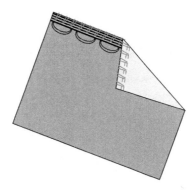

7. Flip the elastic to the back side of the garment. The decorative edge should be the only part visible on the face side of the garment.

8. With the elastic flipped, stitch in place with either a zigzag stitch or a cover stitch.

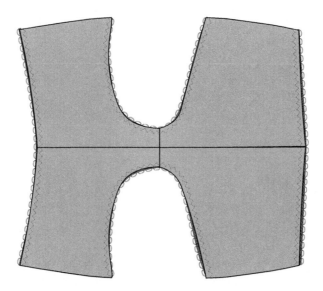

9. Stitch the side seams together, lining up the elastic trim at the top and bottom edges. Pin to secure, or create a hand basted stitch to position the edges precisely.

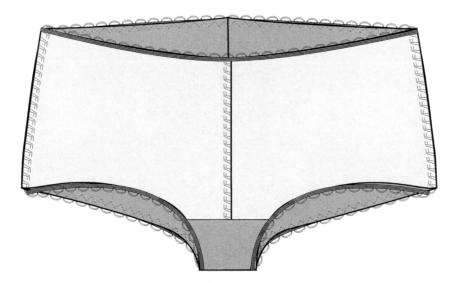

10. If using an overlock stitch, secure the two ends by folding the seam allowance down to one side and backstitching the seam down. Overlock stitches will unravel without a reinforced stitch.

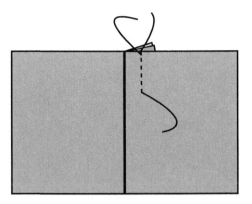

CHAPTER 3

SIDE SEAM ALTERATION FOR A BOYSHORT

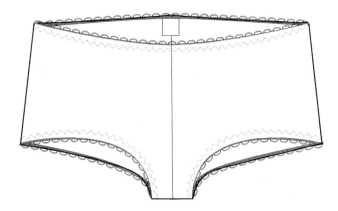

There are instances in which a pattern side seam needs to be eliminated. For this exercise, the side seam shaping is removed to turn the front and back pattern pieces into a single pattern piece. With the elimination of the side seam, an alternative method of elastic attachment is required.

PART 1: PATTERN MANIPULATION

1. Draw in the seam allowance on the front and back, at the side seam. The seam allowance on the provided patterns is 1/4" or 6 mm.

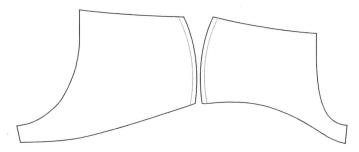

2. To eliminate the side seam, the seam allowances and the curve from the side seam are removed. At the top of the waistline curved side seam, draw a straight line to the lower leg curved side seam, as pictured.

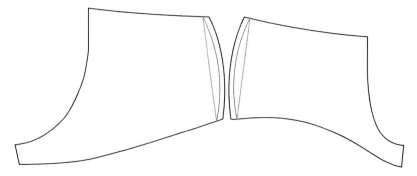

3. Cut the pattern pieces apart on the straight line and attach the patterns at the new side seam. The new side seam becomes the new grainline for the pattern.

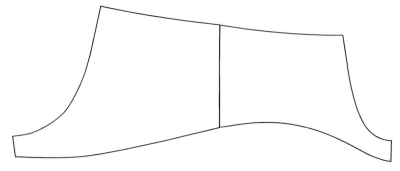

PART 2: CONSTRUCTION METHOD

This exercise introduces a different method in which to attach elastic to the waistline and legs. These steps also show how to conceal a garment label in the waistline of the garment.

1. Cut one right and one left side of the pattern. Cut and prepare the lining as previously demonstrated. With the front sides of the pattern pieces facing each other, attach the curved center seams together.

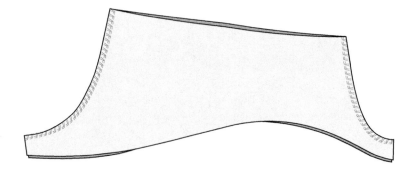

2. Align the center seams together, with the front sides still facing each other. Line up the fabric at the lower crotch seam. Sew together.

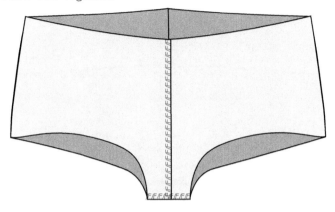

3. Line the center notches on the lining to the center seam. Baste stitch the lining in place along the edges, using a straight stitch.

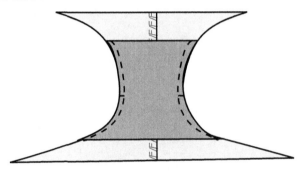

4. Place the elastic around the waistline and leg openings on the face side of the garment. Place the overlapped elastic at the center back and near the crotch seam to hide the overlap. Place the elastic edges at a criss cross angle facing off the raw edge of the fabric.

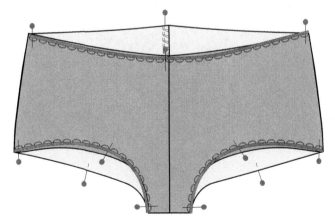

5. Attach the elastic to the garment as previously demonstrated. To add a garment label, stitch the label at the center back. This allows the raw edge of the label to be hidden in the fold in Step 6.

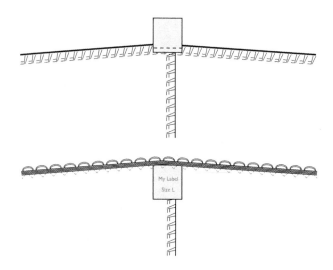

6. Flip the elastic to the back side of the fabric and finish as previously demonstrated.

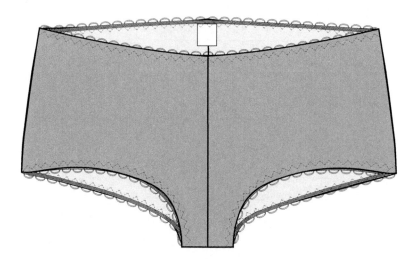

CHAPTER 4
WIDE LACE BOYSHORT

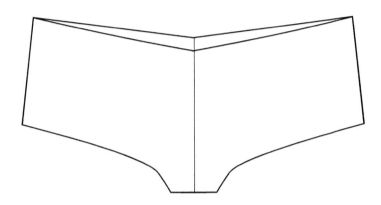

A simplified boyshort design can be created for a wide stretch lace. The pattern utilizes a single pattern piece for the front and back. Follow the steps in Chapter 3 to create a single pattern piece. Laces from 5" to 7" (12 cm to 18 cm) are appropriate for this style. This style is meant to be "cheeky," offering very little coverage on the lower buttocks.

PART 1: PATTERN MANIPULATION

1. Mark the seam allowance of 1/4" or 6 mm up from the crotch/leg point, on both the front and the back sides. This is to indicate where the seam line ends and the seam allowance begins. Seam allowance is not needed on the legs, as the lace has a finished edge and no elastic is added.

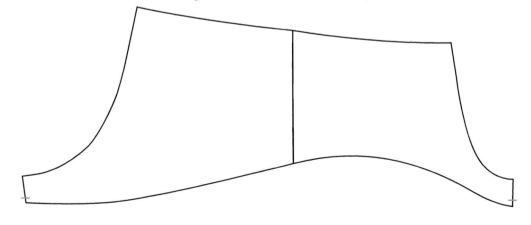

2. Draw a straight line across the boyshort, connecting the 1/4" or 6 mm marks drawn in the previous step.

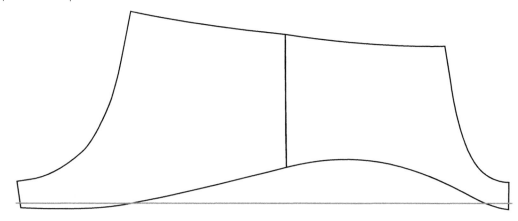

3. Draw a second line, parallel to the bottom line, in the width of the chosen lace.

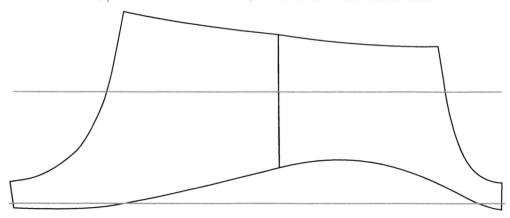

4. The portion of the boy short pattern between the parallel lines becomes the new pattern. The straight lines at the top and bottom of the new pattern piece align to the edges of the wide lace.

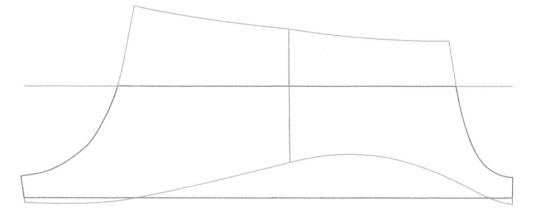

5. The width of the lining needs to match the new pattern piece. At the leg openings, remove the seam allowance of 1/4" or 6 mm.

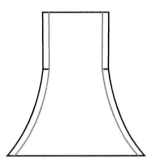

PART 2: CONSTRUCTION METHOD

1. Place the face sides of the lace pattern pieces together. Stitch the center curves on both the front and the back.

2. Align the center seams with the face sides together. Stitch the lower crotch seam together.

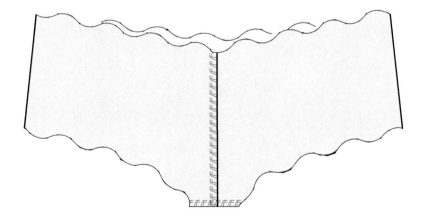

3. Prepare the lining as previously demonstrated. Pin the lining in place, matching the notches to the center seam. Attach the lining to the panty. A zigzag stitch is appropriate for this attachment.

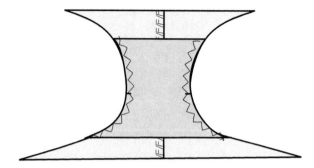

4. If the seams are overlocked, reinforce the ends of the seams at the center front and back by folding the seam to the side and straight stitching.

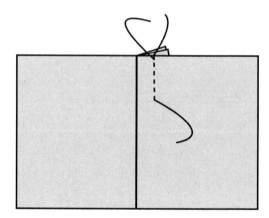

CHAPTER 5

BASIC BRIEF CONSTRUCTION

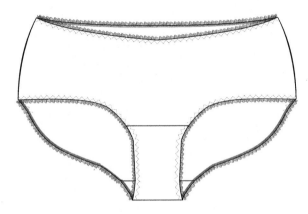

The basic brief provided in the back of this book is comprised of three pattern pieces - the front, back, and lining. Cut and prepare the front pattern piece, back pattern piece, and two linings, with one being in the fashion fabric. One lining faces the body and one faces the outside of the garment. Construction is shown with a ruffle elastic trim.

1. Place the front and lining pieces together. Line up at the front crotch seam with front sides facing each other. Place the second lining on the opposite side of the front, with the face side facing the back side of the front. Attach the front seams together. The front of the brief is sandwiched between the two linings.

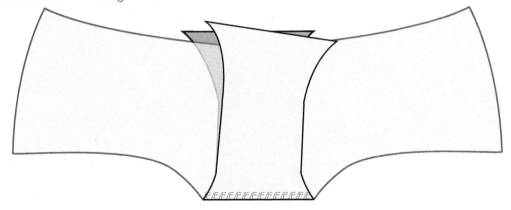

2. There are two options in completing the back seam.

> **Option A** – Take the back and attach it to the two edges of the linings. This makes a visible seam on the inside of the panty.

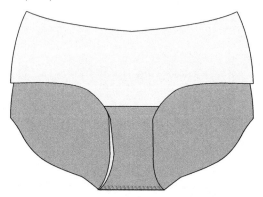

> **Option B** – Take the back and attach the fashion fabric lining at the back crotch seam.

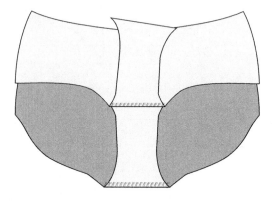

Pull the interior lining over the entire panty to the back side of the back. This is referred to as a burrito roll. Attach the interior lining to the back seam. Pull the fabric through one of the openings. This leaves a clean finish on both the front and back as pictured below.

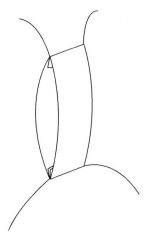

3. Baste the edges of the lining pieces together. This keeps the fabric from moving while attaching the elastic.

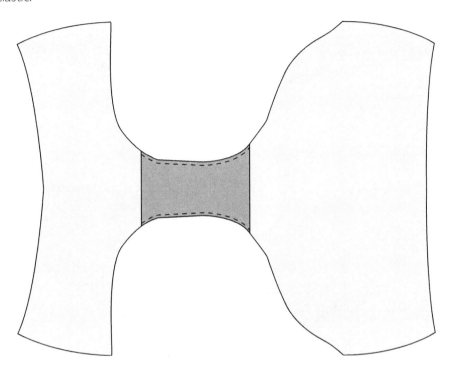

4. Align the elastic trim around the legs and waistline with the decorative edge facing the front side of the fabric. Attach the elastic as previously demonstrated.

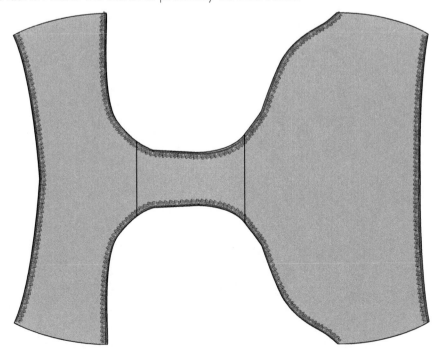

5. Stitch the side seams together and reinforce the beginning and end of the stitch as previously demonstrated. To ensure that the beginning and ending of the stitches line up, pin carefully or hand baste the edges for accuracy.

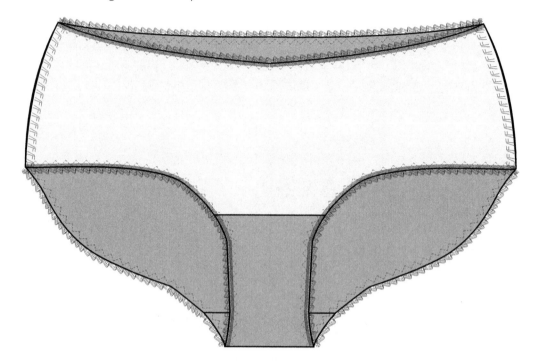

CHAPTER 6

FRONT SEAM ALTERATION FOR A BRIEF

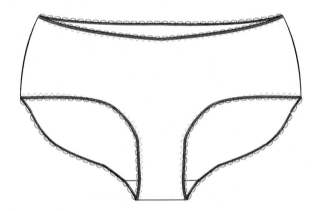

Not all designers wish to have a fully finished lining. Some designers prefer the front to be continuous without a seam with the lining portion loose on the inside. This method of keeping the lining separate makes hand washing easier for spot cleaning. These sewing instructions detail an alternative method of attaching the elastic trim so the full elastic is visible on the outside of the garment.

PART 1: PATTERN MANIPULATION

1. On the front pattern piece, draw in the 1/4" or 6 mm seam allowance at the front crotch seam. Copy the lining pattern. Repeat this step for the copy of the lining pattern piece at the front seam.

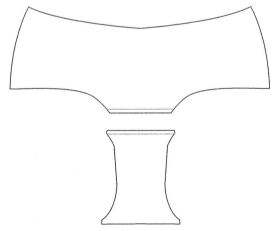

2. Line up the pattern pieces and attach the pattern pieces at the front seam.

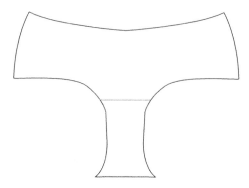

3. For this alternative method of attaching the elastic, the legs and waistline should not have any seam allowance. Alter the pattern by trimming 1/4" or 6 mm off the legs and waistline only.

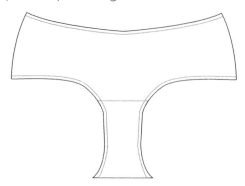

PART 2: CONSTRUCTION METHOD

1. Place the face sides of the front and back pattern pieces together, then place the face side of the lining to the back side of the back. Stitch this seam together, enclosing the lining edge between the front and back pieces.

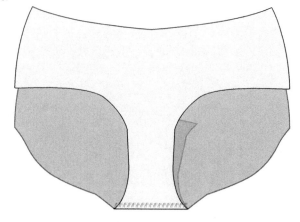

2. Finish the top edge of the lining as previously demonstrated. Flip the lining to clean finish the back seam and baste stitch the lining in place on the sides. This will keep the fabric from moving during the elastic attachment.

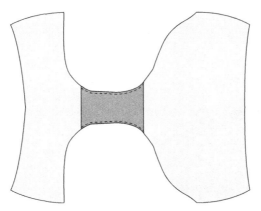

3. Place the side seams together, with the face side of the front lined up to the face side of the back. Stitch the side seams together.

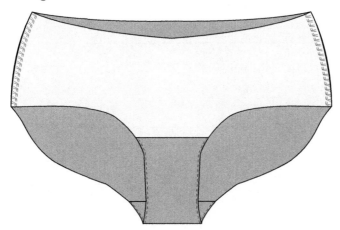

4. Measure the waistline and leg openings along the edges of the paper pattern. Add 1/2" or 12 mm to each measurement. Cut an elastic for the waistline and two leg elastics. Place each elastic together to create a complete circle stitching the ends together as pictured.

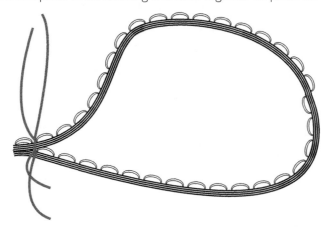

5. Pin to the face side of the garment with the decorative edge hanging off the edge and the seam of the elastic touching the face side of the garment. This is a lapped seam and covers the raw edge of the fabric with the elastic.

When aligning the elastic, be sure that the raw edges of the elastic ends are facing the right the side of the garment.

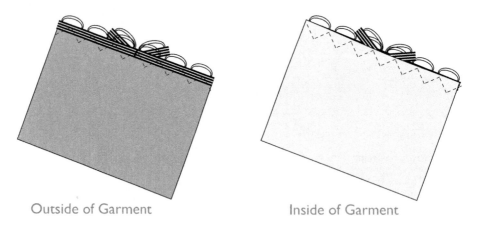

Outside of Garment   Inside of Garment

6. Stitch in place as previously demonstrated.

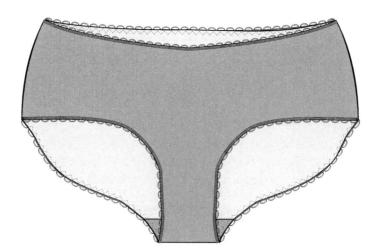

INTERMEDIATE

CHAPTER 7

INTRODUCTION TO PATTERN MANIPULATION

The Intermediate section highlights how to perform more complex pattern alterations. These alterations include creating slopers, changing patterns for fit, creating simple style line changes and adding design details.

TOOLS

French curve – A French curve is used for making small and tightly curved shapes. The French curve is ideal for leg curves and style lines.

Hip or Vary Form curve – A hip curve or vary form curve is needed for longer and gradual curves, typically used for waistlines and side seams.

SUPPLIES

Fold Over Elastic – Fold over elastic (also referred to as FOE) is knitted with a thin seam down the center. It is designed to fold over the edge of fabric to create a clean finish to a raw edge. This elastic stretches when sewn and may not retain its full stretch integrity. Sewing with fold over elastic generally requires the elastic to be slightly stretched when sewn.

Plain or Lingerie Elastic – Plain elastic is self contained in the fold of the fabric on a garment. Lingerie elastic has the same properties as a plain elastic but is plush and can be sewn so the face of the elastic touches the skin.

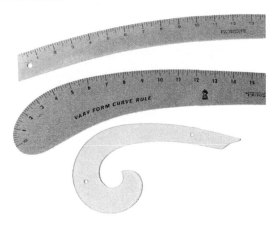

Stretch Lace – Stretch lace trims can come in a variety of different widths, as narrow as 3/8" or 10 mm to as wide as 10" or 25 cm.

It is always recommended to sew a sample of the elastic or lace on a sample of the fabric to determine how the two materials work together.

Oaktag, Manila or Hard Tag Paper – Depending on where one is in the world, this may have different names. This paper is thick, like poster board, and generally manila in color. It is used to finalize patterns and is used for creating slopers. Alternatively, use poster board if there is not access to tag paper.

SLOPERS

Slopers, or pattern blocks, are created and used for easy pattern manipulation. The advanced section walks one through drafting from measurements, but slopers are introduced in this section. The finalized draft becomes a custom sloper.

The next chapter demonstrates how to take the patterns in the back of this book to create a sloper prior to a custom draft.

The main differences between a pattern and a sloper is that a sloper does not contain seam allowances or styled lines, while a pattern does. Slopers are generally created in a designer's sample size, which is the middle size in a range of sizes offered by a designer.

PATTERNS AND LABELING

A manipulated sloper for a custom design must be finalized with seam allowances and pattern details prior to cutting and sewing.

Patterns are generally labeled with a variety of information including the Style Name, Piece Name, Size, and Cut Number.

Patterns are also marked with grainlines to indicate the length grain of the pattern for proper orientation when cutting. Select notching is also done to indicate sewing lines. Notches can be placed outwards as seen on manufactured patterns or inwards using a pattern notcher.

Excessive inward notching on knits is not advised because seam allowances are rather small and over-notching can result in holes in the garment. This is the main reason notching is not used in this book. A notch is generally used to line up pattern pieces, but most panties do not contain any notches.

PATTERN STYLES

Every pattern change affects the fit of a garment. This can affect where the garment sits on the body and how much it covers. Be sure to test each design for fit and functionality.

STYLIZED PANTIES

The intermediate section introduces changing the style lines of the basic boyshort pattern. These changes include changing the shaping of the legs and waistline and adding decorative seam lines.

In addition to altering the style lines, the design technique of slash and spread is used for gathered details to add interest to an otherwise simple brief.

FRENCH KNICKERS

French knickers are a style also known as a tap pant. This design is generally fitted at the waistline but loose at the legs.

STRING BIKINI

A string bikini is a high cut altered brief that can be tied on the side with strings. This design can be adapted to have a fixed separate elastic or lace waistline.

CHAPTER 8

CREATE A SLOPER FROM A PATTERN

A sloper is a base pattern that is designed for a set of measurements and does not include seam allowances. Slopers in both apparel and lingerie design are created with both measurements and specific properties of fabrics in mind. In the case of these patterns, that property is stretch.

Slopers are used often and need a stabilized backing for keeping the integrity of the sloper shape. Sloper drafts can be traced onto a card stock or tag paper for repetitive use. Creating slopers for pattern modifications makes the manipulation of the designs easier to facilitate. Utilize the boyshort and brief patterns from the back of this book to practice your manipulations.

BOYSHORT

1. Draw in the 1/4" or 6 mm seam allowance around all edges of the front, back and lining.

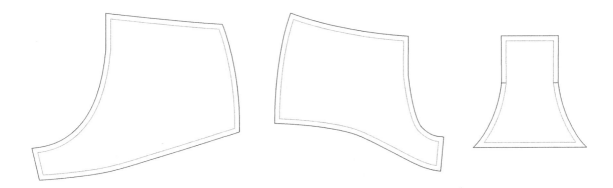

2. Remove the seam allowances and match each seam to check for inaccuracies in cutting seam allowances. Be sure to match side seams and center crotch seams. Make adjustments as necessary. The easiest method to do this is to line up the patterns on top of each other. The side seam pictured below is equal and matches perfectly.

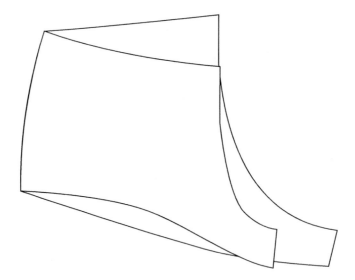

3. Once finalized, stabilize the sloper pattern by stapling or tracing onto tag paper. Label each pattern piece with the sloper name, piece name, size and the stretch used to create the sloper. The patterns provided in the back of this book utilize a 50% stretch in the width and a 30% stretch in the height.

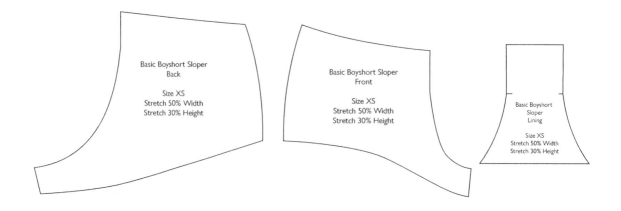

BRIEF

1. Draw in the 1/4" or 6 mm seam allowance around all outer edges of the front, back and lining. Do not remove anything from the center front or center back of the pattern pieces. These are placed on the fold.

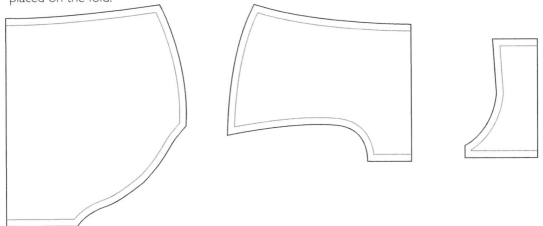

2. Remove the seam allowances and match each seam to check for inaccuracies. Be sure to match side seams and crotch seams exactly. Make adjustments as necessary. The easiest way to do this is to line up the patterns on top of each other. The side seam pictured below is not equal. This shape and length needs to be adjusted to match. This is referered to as "truing the pattern."

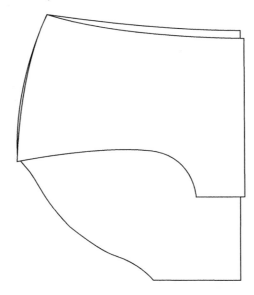

3. Once finalized, stabilize the sloper by stapling or tracing onto tag paper or poster board. Label each piece with the sloper name, piece name, size and the stretch used. The patterns in the back of this book utilize a 50% stretch in the width and a 30% stretch in the height.

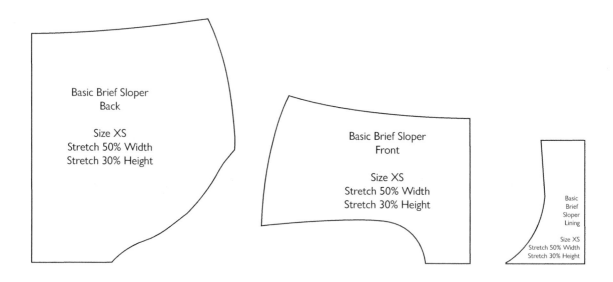

CHAPTER 9
PATTERN DIRECTIONS

In the following chapters, the sloper is utilized to create new designs through a process called pattern manipulation. This chapter shows how to turn drafts into a pattern through the addition of adding seam allowance. Utilize this information for finalizing custom drafts from the Advanced section of the book. For basic practice, take the slopers created in Chapter 8 to create patterns.

BOYSHORT

1. Add seam allowances around all edges of both the boyshort and lining. This amount can be altered, based on preference or construction methods. 1/4" or 6 mm is the minimum required for sewing. 3/8" or 10 mm is the standard seam allowance for stretch garments in the garment industry. Seam allowance may be found up to 5/8" or 15 mm depending on the final user's requirements. Select a seam allowance for these patterns. Be sure to indicate the seam allowance on each pattern piece.

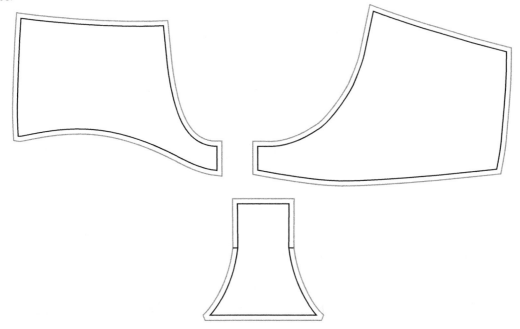

2. a. Label each pattern piece with the pattern name, piece name, size, the cut instructions, and seam allowance.

    b. The grainline for the boyshort is placed in the center of each pattern piece, dividing it in half vertically.

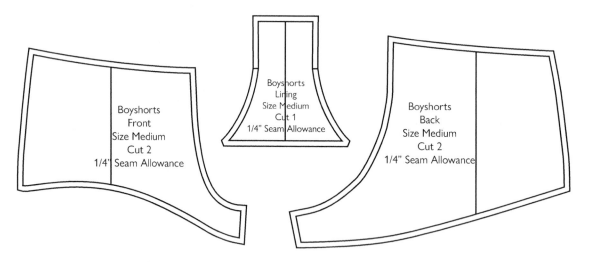

BRIEF

1. Add seam allowances around all edges of both the boyshort and lining, except for the center fold lines. This amount can be altered, based on preference or construction methods. 1/4" or 6 mm is the minimum required for sewing. 3/8" or 10 mm is the standard seam allowance for stretch garments in the garment industry. Seam allowances may be found up to 5/8" or 15 mm depending on the final user's requirements. Select a seam allowance for these patterns. Be sure to indicate the seam allowance on each pattern piece.

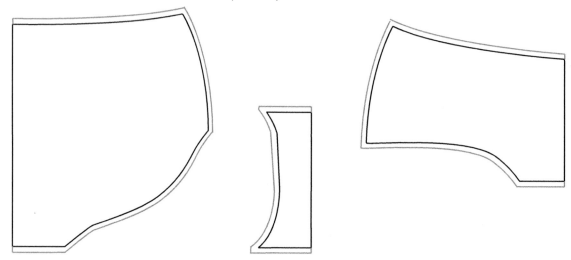

2. a. Label each pattern piece with the pattern name, piece name, size, the cut instructions, and the seam allowance.

  b. The grainline for the brief is placed on the center fold line of each pattern piece, dividing it in half vertically.

  c. The lining pattern piece is utilized for cutting one layer of fashion fabric to match the front and back pattern pieces and one layer of lining for the inside of the panty.

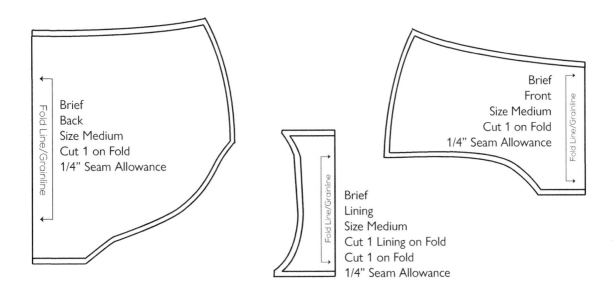

Brief
Back
Size Medium
Cut 1 on Fold
1/4" Seam Allowance

Fold Line/Grainline

Brief
Lining
Size Medium
Cut 1 Lining on Fold
Cut 1 on Fold
1/4" Seam Allowance

Fold Line/Grainline

Brief
Front
Size Medium
Cut 1 on Fold
1/4" Seam Allowance

Fold Line/Grainline

CHAPTER 10

ALTERING PATTERNS TO FIT

ANATOMICAL ADJUSTMENTS

Not all panty designs fit all body shapes, but not in ways you might think. The shape of a person's pelvis can affect how underpants fit. While a custom draft is always the best way to have a perfect fit, one often wants to utilize ready-made patterns and cute designs that are already available.

Patterns are designed around a fit model or the pattern maker's ideal customer; this includes the crotch length, depth and width. The same goes for the patterns provided in the back of this book. These measurements were developed based on a set of average measurements.

What if your pelvic shape is drastically different than that of the drafted pattern? There are four basic skeletal pelvic shapes: Anthropoid, Gynecoid, Android and Platypelloid. These are Greek terms and were documented by two scientists in the 1930s. Individuals defined with a Gynecoid or Platypelloid pelvic shape have a wider space between their legs, approximately 2 1/2" or 6.35 cm, while the Android and the Anthropoid spacing is approximately 2" or 5 cm. These variations can cause significant changes to how a panty fits. The illustration below helps to show those pelvic differences.

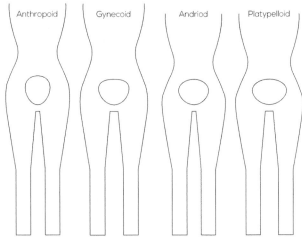

Anthropoid   Gynecoid   Andriod   Platypelloid

The categorization of these pelvic shapes was created by William Edgar Caldwell and Howard Carmen Moloy in 1933-1934, to help doctors determine whether a woman could successfully deliver a child vaginally. While these categorizations are no longer what doctors depend on, it helps explain the differences in body shapes and how panties fit. The bodies below are all considered a medium, but the panty that fits the body on the left is the only one that fits properly.

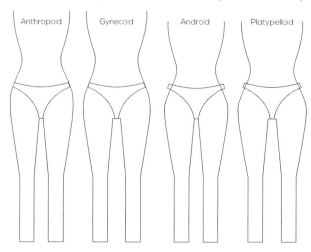

The Gynecoid and Platypelloid would be uncomfortable as the crotch width is not wide enough to stay in position. The Android and the Platypelloid would have an issue of the panty sitting too high on the body and the crotch length being too long, causing the panty to ride up in the back.

With the vast differences of an individuals' anatomies and the patterns that are available, adjustments may be required to shorten/lengthen the crotch and/or to narrow/widen the lining pattern. The alterations could be any combination based on the designer's base pattern and the body shape and size that the pattern was designed for.

To alter a pattern that cuts into the front leg crease, meaning the coverage is too great, alterations may be needed to narrow the crotch width and/or extend the crotch length. This panty may have been designed for an individual defined with a Platypelloid shape.

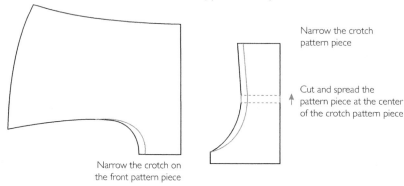

Narrow the crotch on the front pattern piece

Narrow the crotch pattern piece

Cut and spread the pattern piece at the center of the crotch pattern piece

To alter a pattern that doesn't cover the full crotch width, alterations may be to widen the crotch width or shorten the crotch length. This pattern may have been designed for an individual defined with an Anthropoid shape.

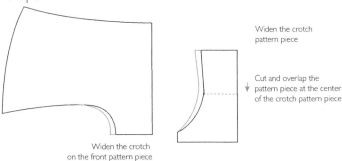

Widen the crotch
pattern piece

Cut and overlap the
pattern piece at the center
of the crotch pattern piece

Widen the crotch
on the front pattern piece

PHYSICAL ADJUSTMENTS

Physical differences in our anatomy may not be bone related, but can still cause clothes to not fit properly. These differences can be muscle- or fat-related in nature. A muscular individual has fit issues that an overweight individual may not.

Muscles can cause garments to move more aggressively with average movements. An individual with the same measurements as someone muscular, but who has minimal muscular development, may not have these issues because the tissue is soft.

There is no such thing as a "normal" body, but designers create their patterns for the "normal" figure of their customer. This customer can be curvy, flat, muscular or overweight, which causes patterns to require adjustments for fit.

For underpants that sag in the back, an adjustment to shorten the back of the pattern may be necessary. This can be achieved by taking a dart out of the back in the amount the pattern sags. On the pattern piece, close the dart, straighten the center back line and adjust the back crotch line to be perpendicular to the center back line. This pattern may have been designed for an individual with a rounder backside.

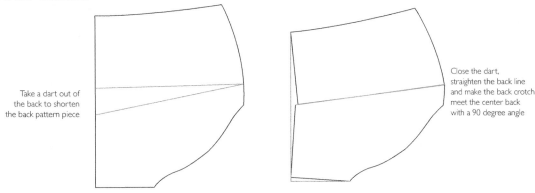

Take a dart out of
the back to shorten
the back pattern piece

Close the dart,
straighten the back line
and make the back crotch
meet the center back
with a 90 degree angle

For underpants that cut into the buttocks, lengthen the crotch at the back seam and add more height to the back pattern piece. This pattern may have been designed for an individual with a flat backside.

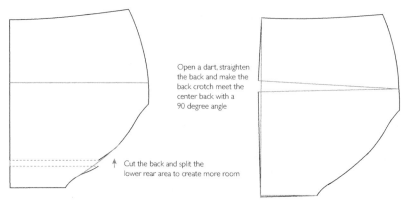

Open a dart, straighten the back and make the back crotch meet the center back with a 90 degree angle

Cut the back and split the lower rear area to create more room

Some patterns may need what is termed as a full seat or a full butt adjustment. This adjustment can be to create a dart on the side seam in the back but not adding height to the panty. A dart will need to be sewn on the panty design. This pattern is adjusted for a very voluptuous rear end.

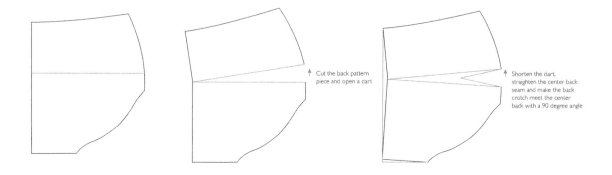

Cut the back pattern piece and open a dart

Shorten the dart, straighten the center back seam and make the back crotch meet the center back with a 90 degree angle

CHAPTER 11

STYLIZING A BOYSHORT: SEAM LINES

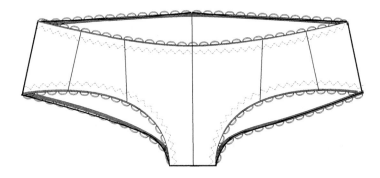

Creating seam lines or style lines is a technique to add interest to a simple design. They can be used to add color blocking or lace inserts into the design.

PART 1: PATTERN MANIPULATION

1. Trace the front and back boyshort slopers, by lining up the front and back slopers at the waist/side seam point and the leg/side seam point. This removes the curved side seam and creates a pattern without a side seam.

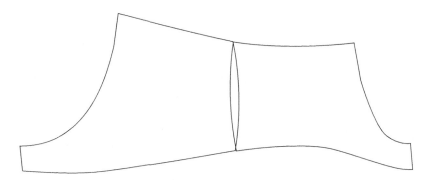

2. Design and modify the waistline shape and leg opening shape. A portion of the curve from the back leg is removed to create a "cheeky" back. The front leg is cut higher for more of a bikini cut. The waistline is lowered to create a low rise front.

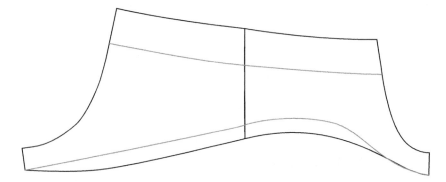

3. Create a seam line based on design preference. This can be a single seam to offset the front from the back, or multiple seams for design aesthetics. In this example, a separate panel is created for contrast fabric.

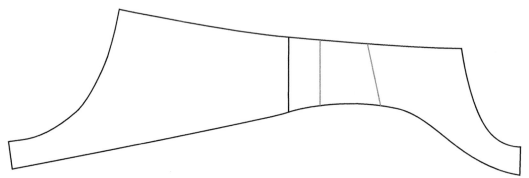

4. Cut and separate the pattern.

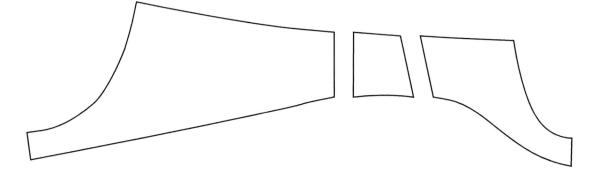

5. Alterations to the shaping of the leg requires a minor alteration to the lining sloper.

    a. On the front crotch/leg point, measure 1 3/4" or 4.5 cm towards the back seam on the leg curve. Draw a 90 degree angle towards the center front curve and measure the width.

    b. On the back, measure 3 1/2" or 9 cm towards the front. Draw a 90 degree angle towards the center back curve and measure the width of that line.

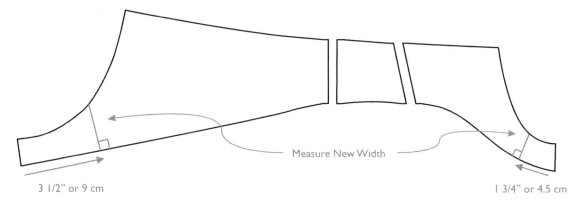

Measure New Width

3 1/2" or 9 cm   1 3/4" or 4.5 cm

6. Record the measurements from the front and back.

    a. Trace the lining sloper.

    b. Alter the pattern piece where necessary. This example changes the back width but has no effect on the front.

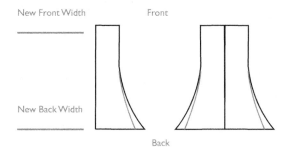

New Front Width   Front

New Back Width

Back

7. Add seam allowances to all pattern pieces as per the instructions in Chapter 9. Complete the pattern by adding the pattern information.

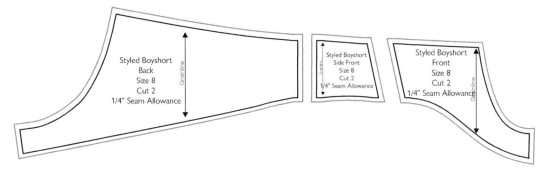

Styled Boyshort
Back
Size 8
Cut 2
1/4" Seam Allowance

Styled Boyshort
Side Front
Size 8
Cut 2
1/4" Seam Allowance

Styled Boyshort
Front
Size 8
Cut 2
1/4" Seam Allowance

PART 2: CONSTRUCTION METHOD

1. Align the pattern pieces, with the face sides toward each other. At the fabric edge, sew together.

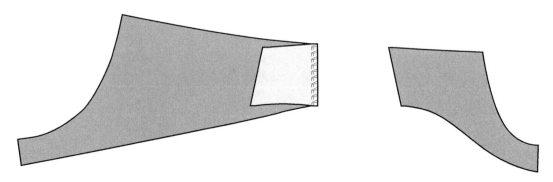

2. Attach the remaining pattern piece with face sides together. Complete the construction of the boyshort as previously demonstrated.

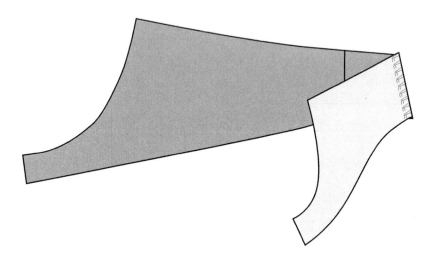

CHAPTER 12

STYLIZING A BOYSHORT: SLASH AND SPREAD

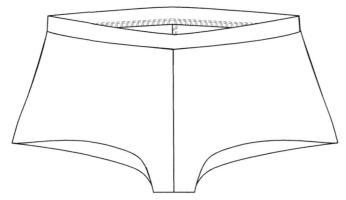

French knickers, also known as a tap pant, resemble shorts, with a fitted waistline and an open or loose fitting leg. These knickers are usually decorated with lace, but can also be made from cotton for a more casual design. The method of pattern manipulation to create this design is referred to as slash and spread.

PART 1: PATTERN MANIPULATION

1. Trace the front and back boyshort sloper pieces. Measure the waistline of the front and the back. Record these measurements below. This amount can also be recorded directly on the sloper pieces for future reference.

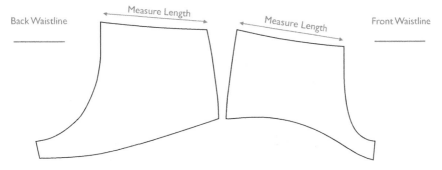

2. Divide each of the boyshort body pieces into four equal parts. Cut both the front and back out and slash from the bottom up, leaving it attached at the top edge.

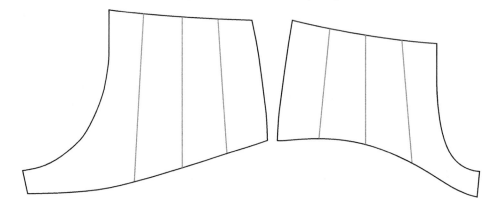

3. Spread the cut panels evenly at the hemline and secure to a second piece of paper. This method of pattern manipulation is referred to as slash and spread. Tape the cut pattern pieces down.

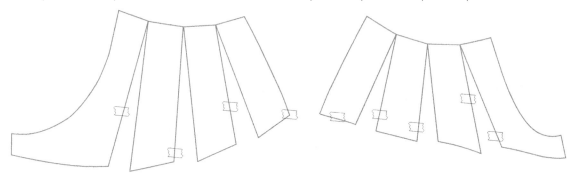

4. Use the curved ruler to create a smooth line. For the pieces in the center of the pattern body, take the average of each shape and make a smooth blended curve.

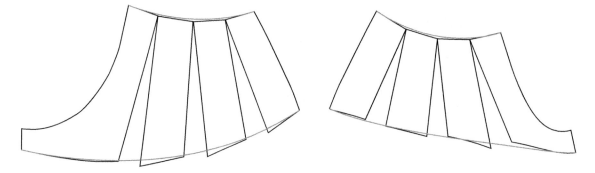

5. The grainline can be at the designer's discretion, depending on the desired drape on the body. Complete these patterns by adding seam allowance and pattern information.

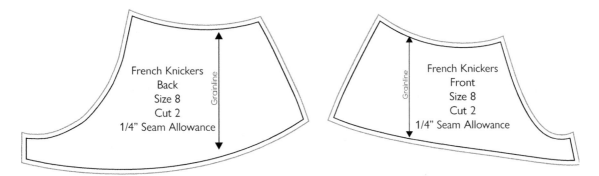

6. For this style, a separate waistband is created to house the elastic. Two separate waistband pattern pieces are created, one for the front and one for the back. Double both measurements to arrive at the full front and back amounts. On a separate paper, draw a line in the amount of the Full Front Waistline.

Front Sloper Measurement		Back Sloper Measurement	
	× 2		× 2
Full Front Waistline		Full Back Waistline	

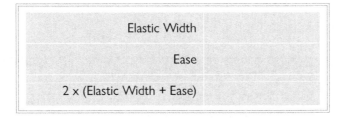

Full Front Waistline

7. To determine the waistband height take the width of the preferred elastic, and add 1/8" or 3 mm to the width measurement, for pattern ease. Multiply the total by two to create the fold over amount of the encased waistband.

Elastic Width	
Ease	
2 × (Elastic Width + Ease)	

8. Square a line up at both ends of the waistband front, in the amount determined in the previous step.

9. Add seam allowances around the edges, in the amount that corresponds to the construction method required. Repeat this process for the back waistband. Complete the pattern piece with pattern information.

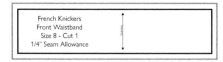

PART 2: CONSTRUCTION METHOD

1. Construct the body of the panty as previously demonstrated for the boyshorts. Attach the center curves and the side seams. Sew the crotch seam together and baste the lining in place before proceeding to the following steps.

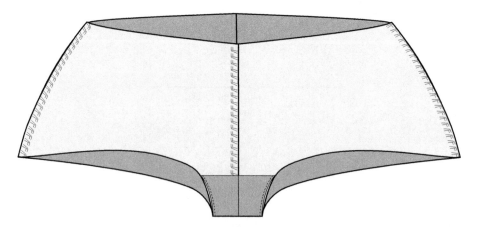

2. Attach the front and back waistband at the side seams.

3. To determine the length of elastic needed, add the full front and full back waistline measurements together, then add 1" or 25 mm for sewing allowance. Sew the elastic together at the ends to complete a full circle. Due to the thickness of waistband elastic, overlap the elastic by 1/2" or 12.5 mm on both sides and stitch in the middle.

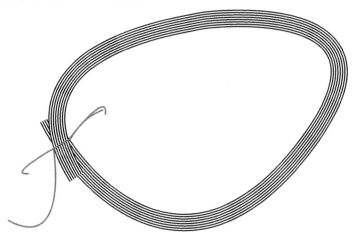

4. Fold the waistband over the elastic, with the wrong side of the waistband facing the elastic.

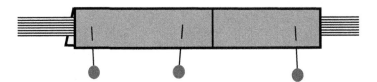

5. Pin the raw edges of the waistband to the waistline of the knickers with the band on the face side of the garment. Attach the waistband to the waistline.

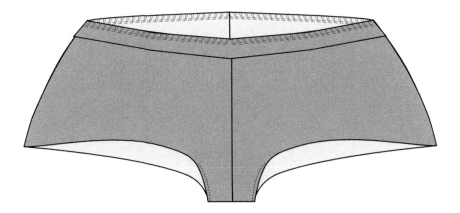

6. A rolled hem, or merrow edge finish, stretches the edge of the fabric for a ruffled look. For a traditional hem, fold and stitch.

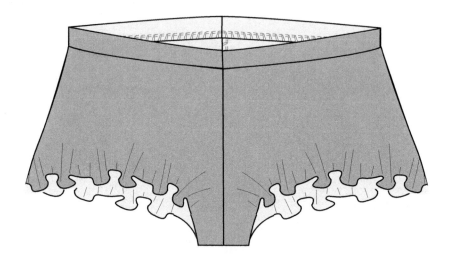

CHAPTER 13

STYLIZING A BRIEF: CUT OUTS

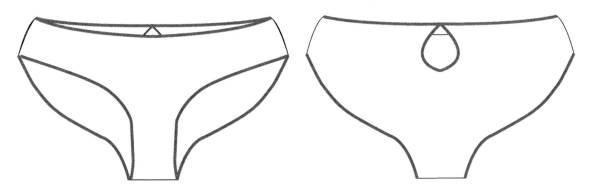

This lesson demonstrates how to change the brief into a bikini style, with the addition of a keyhole cut out in the back for design detail. Construction steps provide instructions for utilizing fold over elastic.

PART 1: PATTERN MANIPULATION

1. Trace the front, back, and lining sloper pieces. Align the lining piece to the front, creating a single front pattern piece.

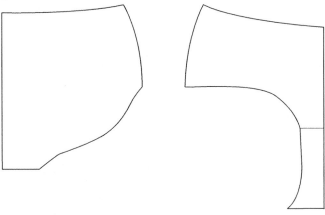

2. Alter the waistline and leg opening for design preference. A bikini cut is generally higher on the hip than a brief. Be sure to check that the side seams on the front and back remain equal in length and line up. Create a smooth transition from the front to the back.

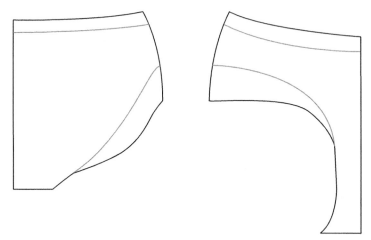

3. Create the keyhole cutout in the back, all the way up to the waistline.

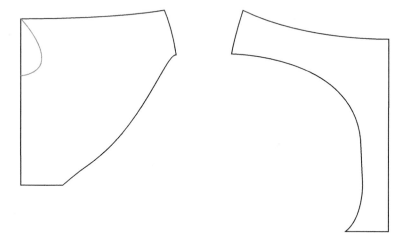

4. Add seam allowances to the side seams and crotch seams only. Fold over elastic utilizes the seam line edge and does not require a seam allowance. Adding seam allowances would make the pattern too large around the waistline and leg openings. Complete the pattern with pattern information.

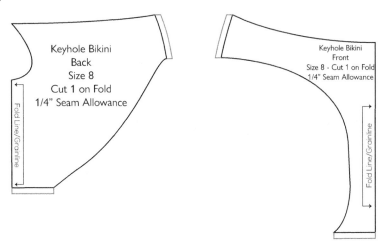

PART 2: CONSTRUCTION METHOD

1. To finish this keyhole shape, select a fold over elastic. This elastic is ideal for finishing the raw edge of the fabric. Fold over elastic is rather difficult to sew and can be hard to control at first use. Iron the elastic on the fold prior to sewing to assist in the attachment process. Place the elastic over the edge of the keyhole opening and stitch with a stretch stitch, slightly pulling the elastic while sewing. It is recommended to test the elastic on a sample prior to sewing with good fabric.

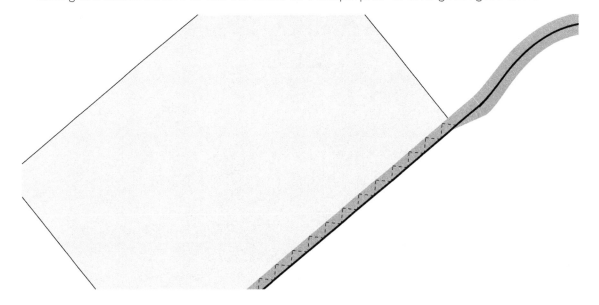

2. Attach the elastic to the waistline and leg openings. Overlap the fold over elastic in an inconspicuous location. This can be at the side seam and in the crotch area. To clean finish the overlap, clip the beginning of the attached fold over elastic at an angle. Clip the other end into an outward facing V and fold under just past the overlap.

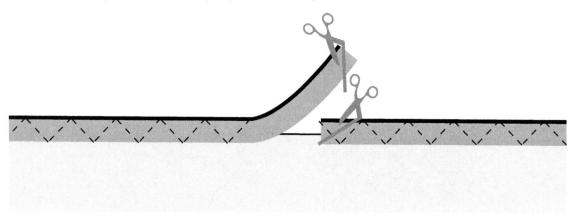

3. Be sure to line up the keyhole cut out at the edges and complete with fold over elastic on all edges.

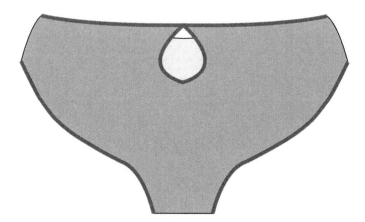

CHAPTER 14

STYLIZING A BRIEF: SLASH AND SPREAD

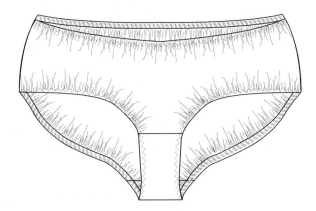

Creating a ruffled or gathered brief is a style that works well with either woven or knit fabrics. The slash and spread method creates fullness in the design that is gathered to create a ruffled knicker design.

PART 1: PATTERN MANIPULATION

1. Trace the brief sloper pieces. Measure the waistline of the front and back, and the leg opening of the front, back, and lining. These amounts can be recorded below and/or directly on the sloper.

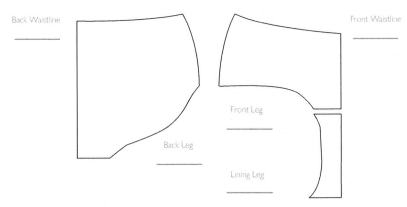

2. To create allover fullness, the brief is cut and spread, then gathered back to the original shape, creating a gathered or ruffled panty design.

    a. Draw a line from the middle of the crotch seam, straight up to the waistline.

    b. Divide the remainder of the body into equal parts.

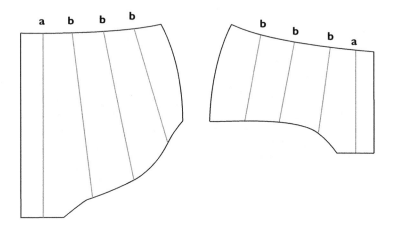

3. Prepare a piece of paper and establish the grainlines on the far right and left of the paper.

    a. Determine the amount of gathering preferred. In this example, each panel is spread by 1" or 25 mm. Gathering is needed at the center front and back of the waistline for an equally gathered look. The top of the center is positioned at 1/2 of the determined spread. In this case, it is 1/2" or 12.5 mm.

    b. Align the center front and the center back crotch points at the grainlines.

    c. On the line closest to the center, slash down from the waist towards the crotch seam. Do not separate; the crotch width does not change.

    d. Spread the line drawn for step c, the full 1" or 25 mm and secure in place.

    e. Draw a line across the patterns, approximately 1" or 25 mm below the waistline.

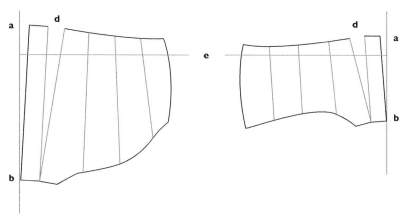

4. **a.** Number the remainder of the panels in order to realign the pattern pieces correctly.

b. Slash the remaining pieces all the way through, from top to bottom.

c. Draw in the guideline across the paper that was drawn on the pattern pieces.

d. Spread the panels by the full spread amount and line up each piece to the horizontal guideline, in order to keep the shape of the garment. Secure in place.

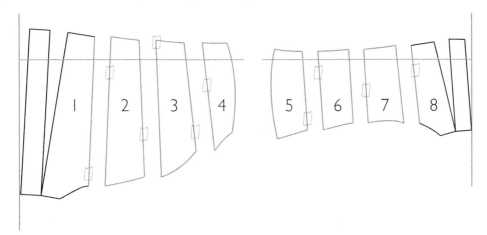

5. Draw the new waist and leg openings using a French or hip curve. Create an average shape of the points to make a smooth curved line.

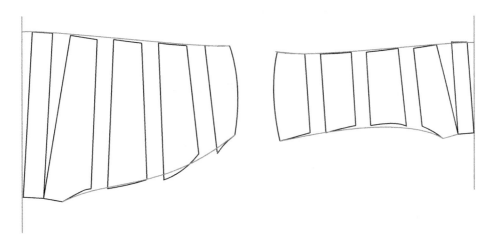

6. Because the width of the pattern was altered, the original measurements are utilized to determine the elastic length.

    a. Use the chart below to transfer the original measurements taken in step 1.

    b. Add the front and back waist measurements to equal the full waist measurement.

    c. Add the front and back leg measurements to the lining leg measurement to equal the full leg measurements.

    d. Add 1" or 25 mm to each measurement, for the seam allowance. The elastic is overlapped and sewn at 1/2" or 12.5 mm seam allowance.

    e. Cut one piece of elastic for the waistline and two for the legs.

WAIST MEASUREMENTS

Front Waist Measurement	
Back Waist Measurement	+
Full Waist Measurement	=
Add Seam Allowance	+
Elastic Length	=

LEG MEASUREMENTS

Front Leg Measurement	
Back Leg Measurement	+
Lining Leg Measurement	+
Full Leg Measurement	=
Add Seam Allowance	+
Elastic Length	=

7. Add seam allowance around all seam edges as previously demonstrated. Complete the pattern with pattern information.

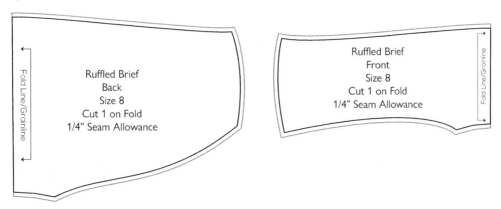

PART 2: CONSTRUCTION METHOD

1. Attach the front, back, and lining pieces as previously demonstrated.

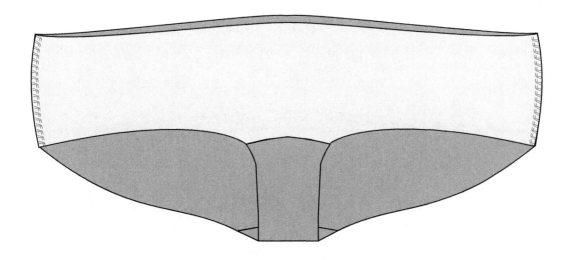

VARIATION A: RUFFLED EDGE FINISH

2. For this method, create a rolled hem or merrow edge finish around all exposed raw edges. Follow Variation B for an option to clean finish the waist and legs.

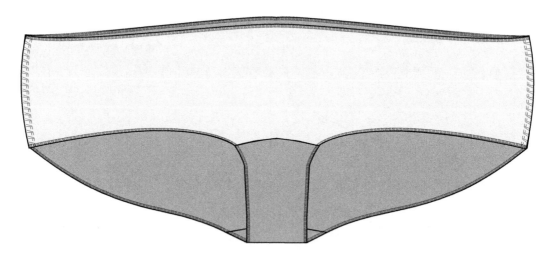

3. Using a plain elastic, sew the ends together as demonstrated in Chapter 12. Stretch the elastic evenly around the waistband and legs, 1/2" or 12.5 mm away from the finished edge. Avoid stretching the elastic at the lining, since this pattern piece was not altered. This image shows the elastic stretched to fit the waistline and leg openings. If the waistline is larger than the elastic will stretch, create a running gathered stitch on the brief prior to attaching the stretched elastic.

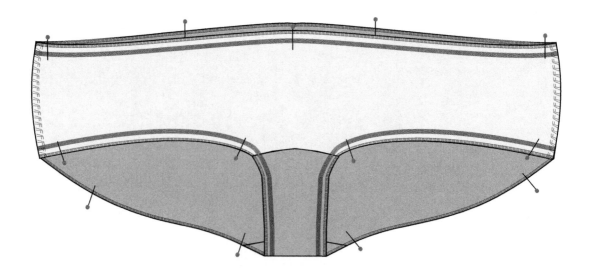

4. Once the elastic is stretched to fit, stitch the elastic with either a straight stitch or zigzag stitch. When the elastic is released from its stretched state, the edges will gather together, as pictured below.

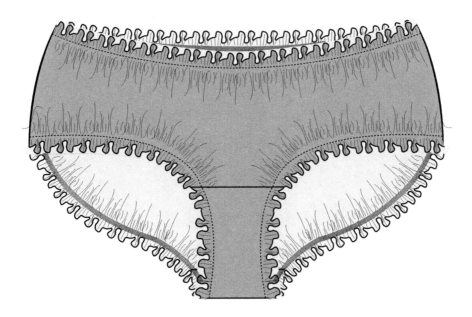

VARIATION B: CLEAN EDGE FINISH

2. Take the elastic and attach the ends of the elastic together at 1/2" or 12.5 mm, as demonstrated in Chapter 12. Stretch the elastic around all edges and attach to the garment, on the back side of the fabric, with either an overlock stitch or zigzag stitch. If the waistline is larger than the elastic will stretch, create a running gathered stitch on the panty, prior to attaching the stretched elastic.

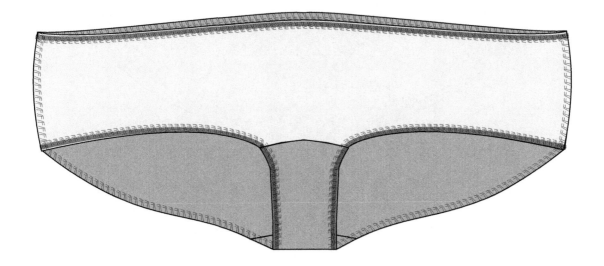

3. Fold over the edge to the back side of the fabric leaving no elastic visible. Pin in place and secure while stretching the elastic.

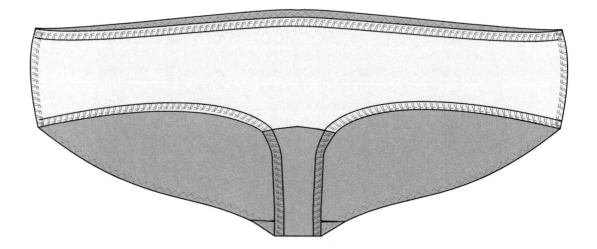

4. Release from the stretched shape to complete the panty as pictured below.

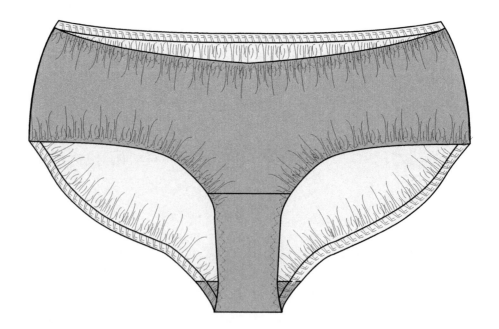

CHAPTER 15

STRING BIKINI WITH LACE

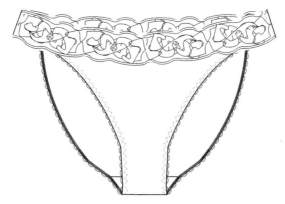

A string bikini is a high cut panty that generally ties at the sides with a string or has a separate waistband. In this example, stretch lace is utilized for the waistband instead of a tie or string.

PART 1: PATTERN MANIPULATION

1. Trace the brief sloper. Align the lining pattern to the front for a combined front.

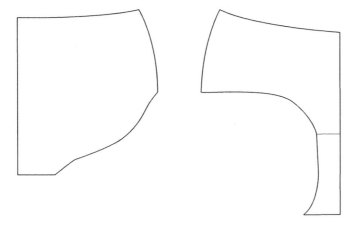

2. Lower the waistline and raise the leg, as pictured. The exact amounts can vary based on preference. At the height at which the side seam of the front ends, match the back to the same height. This will ensure that the garment fit is balanced on the body.

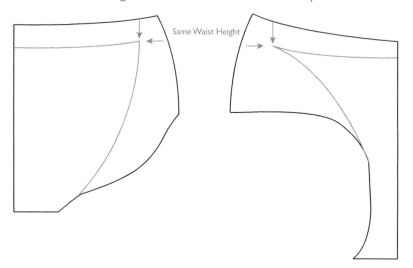

3. a. Measure the front waist of the modified design.

   b. Measure the distance from the new style line to the original side seam.

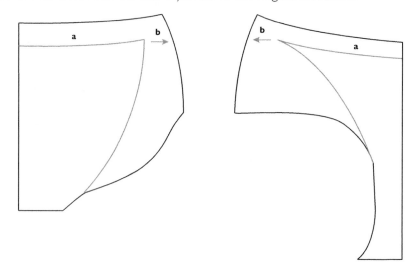

4. a. For the lace waistband, the full waistline amount is required. Total the front & back for a full waistline measurement.

    b. Take the full measurement and add 1" or 25 mm to the length for seam allowance. The lace is seamed at 1/2 of the added amount.

WAIST MEASUREMENTS

Front Waist Measurement	
Front Side Seam Gap	+
Back Waist Measurement	+
Back Side Seam Gap	+
Full Waist Measurement	=
Add Seam Allowance	+
Lace Cut Length	=

5. Trace the front lining area to create a new lining pattern piece.

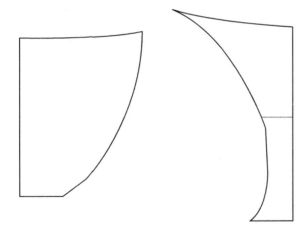

6. Add seam allowance to all pattern pieces as previously demonstrated. Complete the pattern with pattern information.

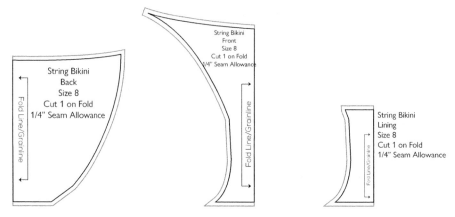

PART 2: CONSTRUCTION METHOD

1. Attach the front, back, and lining pieces as previously demonstrated to finish the lining.

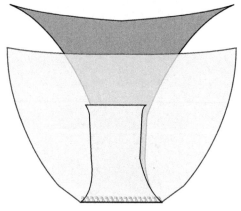

2. Attach decorative elastic to both legs using any of the previously demonstrated attachment methods.

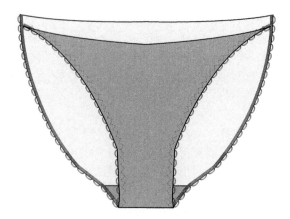

3. Attach the ends of the stretch lace together. Stitch at 1/2" or 12.5 mm seam allowance and crease open.

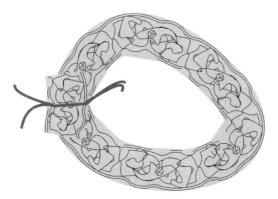

4. Place the lace over the waistline, overlapping the lace on the raw edge by the seam allowance amount added to the waistline. Center the front and back, leaving the same gap on both sides. Place the seam in an inconspicuous location. Attach to the edge by a zigzag stitch or coverstitch.

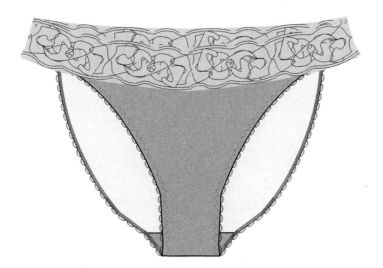

ADVANCED

CHAPTER 16

INTRODUCTION TO PATTERN DRAFTING AND GRADING

The beginner and intermediate sections of this book have introduced several construction and pattern manipulation concepts. The advanced section guides one through the process of drafting a basic boyshort, brief, and thong panty.

TERMINOLOGY

Grading – Grading is the process of creating graduated sizes for a size range.

FABRICS, ELASTICS & STRETCH

In the previous sections, information on stretch for both fabric and elastic was discussed. This section develops the custom draft based on the stretch of the fabrics used. For creating a line of lingerie utilizing multiple types of fabrics with multiple stretch properties, a separately drafted sloper is recommended.

Many fabrics have the same stretch rates as elastics. If elastic stretches more than the fabric, follow the techniques to reduce the elastic measurements discussed later in this chapter. Stretching elastic to fit the pattern will be required.

REDUCING STRETCH

Through extensive testing, reducing the stretch of a fabric by 30% worked well for both fabric and elastics. In the following chart, reductions for 25% and 35% are also provided for reference. This variety of information is provided as each fabric wears differently and may require customizing.

If a fabric stretches 50%, the total stretch cannot be removed or the garment will be skin tight. While this method may work for shape wear, it is not appropriate for panties. 50% stretch is recommended to be reduced by only 30%.

To determine the reduced stretch amounts, take the stretch percentage and multiply by the reduction (i.e. (.5 x .3) = .15) then subtract that amount from 1. The act of reducing the stretch is considered negative ease. The chart below calculates the stretch reduction in an easy to reference manner. The drafting chapters refer to this chart.

The chart on the next page is an example of how to group the stretch amounts of multiple fabrics. This method allows one to create slopers for specific levels of stretch.

Imperial Stretched Amount (inches)	Metric Stretched Amount (centimeters)	Stretch	25% Stretch Multiplier	30% Stretch Multiplier	35% Stretch Multiplier
5 1/4	10 1/2	5%	0.9875	0.985	0.9825
5 1/2	11	10%	0.975	0.97	0.965
5 3/4	11 1/2	15%	0.9625	0.955	0.9475
6	12	20%	0.95	0.94	0.93
6 1/4	12 1/2	25%	0.9375	0.925	0.9125
6 1/2	13	30%	0.925	0.91	0.895
6 3/4	13 1/2	35%	0.9125	0.895	0.8775
7	14	40%	0.9	0.88	0.86
7 1/4	14 1/2	45%	0.8875	0.865	0.8425
7 1/2	15	50%	0.875	0.85	0.825
7 3/4	15 1/2	55%	0.8625	0.835	0.8075
8	16	60%	0.85	0.82	0.79
8 1/4	16 1/2	65%	0.8375	0.805	0.7725
8 1/2	17	70%	0.825	0.79	0.755
8 3/4	17 1/2	75%	0.8125	0.775	0.7375
9	18	80%	0.8	0.76	0.72
9 1/4	18 1/2	85%	0.7875	0.745	0.7025
9 1/2	19	90%	0.775	0.73	0.685
9 3/4	19 1/2	95%	0.7625	0.715	0.6675
10	20	100%	0.75	0.7	0.65
10 1/4	20 1/2	105%	0.7375	0.685	0.6325
10 1/2	21	110%	0.725	0.67	0.615
10 3/4	21 1/2	115%	0.7125	0.655	0.5975
11	22	120%	0.7	0.64	0.58
11 1/4	22 1/2	125%	0.6875	0.625	0.5625
11 1/2	23	130%	0.675	0.61	0.545
11 3/4	23 1/2	135%	0.6625	0.595	0.5275
12	24	140%	0.65	0.58	0.51
12 1/4	24 1/2	145%	0.6375	0.565	0.4925
12 1/2	25	150%	0.625	0.55	0.475
12 3/4	25 1/2	155%	0.6125	0.535	0.4575
13	26	160%	0.6	0.52	0.44

Classification	Imperial Stretched Amounts (inches)	Metric Stretched Amounts (centimeters)	Average Stretch	25% Stretch Multiplier	30% Stretch Multiplier	35% Stretch Multiplier
Little or No Stretch	5.25 to 5.5	10.5 to 11	7.50%	0.9813	0.9775	0.9738
Slightly Stretchy	5.75 to 6.25	11.5 to 13	22.50%	0.9438	0.9325	0.9213
Moderate Stretch	6.5 to 7.5	13.5 to 15	42.50%	0.8938	0.8725	0.8513
Stretchy	7.75 to 8.25	15.5 to 17	62.50%	0.8438	0.8125	0.7813
Very Stretchy	8.5 to 9.5	17.5 to 19	82.50%	0.7938	0.7525	0.7113
Super Stretchy	9.75 to 10.5	19.5 to 21	102.50%	0.7438	0.6925	0.6413

MEASUREMENTS

The following measurements must be taken in a fitted garment, such as a leotard, or taken in undergarments. DO NOT take these measurements wearing thong panties. This provides inaccurate crotch length measurements. Measurements should be snug, but not tight enough to dent the skin.

CIRCUMFERENCE MEASUREMENTS

Waist Measurement – The waist measurement is taken at the natural waist, which is the narrowest point of the body's mid section. This position is located above the belly button.

High Hip Measurement – The high hip measurement is taken directly above the hip bone. This is located below the belly button.

Low Hip Measurement – The low hip measurement is taken around the widest point of the body in the hip area.

HEIGHT MEASUREMENTS

For height measurements, place a tie around the natural waist.

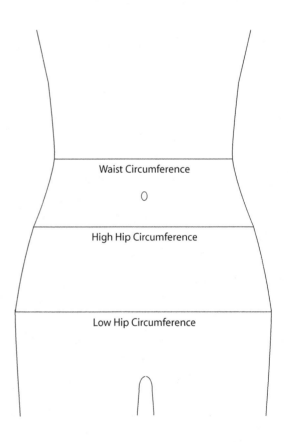

CUSTOM SIZE CHART

Name of Model/Client			
Letter Size		Number Size	
Waist Measurement			
High Hip Measurement		High Hip Depth	
Low Hip Measurement		Low Hip Depth	
Crotch Length		Crotch Depth	

High Hip Depth – Measure from the tie at the natural waistline, to the position in which the high hip circumference was taken, down the center front of the body.

Low Hip Depth – Measure from the tie at the natural waistline, to the position in which the low hip circumference was taken.

Crotch Depth – While sitting on a flat surface (table or chair), measure from the surface to the tie at the natural waist, straight up and not curved to the body.

Crotch Length – To measure the crotch length, measure from the tie at the natural waistline at the center front of the body, between the legs, to the tie at the center back waistline. Be sure the tie does not dip at the center front or center back.

To determine the total crotch amount, double the Crotch Depth and subtract it from the Crotch Length.

Crotch Length	
Crotch Depth x 2	-
Total Crotch Amount	=

To determine the amounts needed for the front and back crotch areas, divide the Total Crotch Amount by 3.

Total Crotch Amount	
Divide by 3	/ 3
1/3 Crotch Amount	=

1/3 of this measurement is the Front Crotch area and 2/3 is the Back Crotch. The crotch is split in this manner for comfort. The back curvature of a woman is generally rounder than the front, accounting for 2/3 of the total crotch measurement.

Front Crotch	
Back Crotch	

GRADING & GRADE RULES

Grading is a term that is used in reference to creating a size range. Grading is a very complicated subject and varies depending on the garment. This book explores the grading methods for both boyshorts and briefs.

When beginning a grade, the size chart must be defined. Utilize the size chart below or create a custom size chart of your own. A size chart

defines the basic grade rules of a garment. It provides the rules on what measurements fit each specified size.

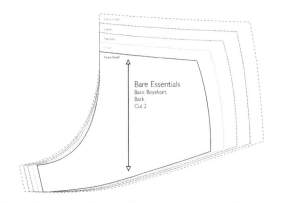

IMPERIAL SIZE CHART
Measurements in Inches

Letter Sizes	XS		S		M		L	
US Number Sizes	0	2	4	6	8	10	12	14
UK Number Sizes	4	6	8	10	12	14	16	18
Waist	22	24	26	28	30	32	34	36
High Hip	28	30	32	34	36	38	40	42
Low Hip	32	34	36	38	40	42	44	46
Crotch Depth	8.5	9	9.5	10	10.5	11	11.5	12
Crotch Length	23.5	24.75	26	27.25	28.5	29.75	31	32.25
Crotch (CL-2CD)	6.5	6.75	7	7.35	7.5	7.75	8	8.25

METRIC SIZE CHART
Measurements in Centimeters

Letter Sizes	XS		S		M		L	
US Number Sizes	0	2	4	6	8	10	12	14
UK Number Sizes	4	6	8	10	12	14	16	18
Waist	56	61	66	71	76	81	86	91
High Hip	71	76	81	86	91	97	102	107
Low Hip	81	86	91	97	102	107	112	117
Crotch Depth	22	23.25	24.5	25.75	27	28.25	29.5	30.75
Crotch Length	59.7	62.86	66.02	69.18	72.34	75.5	78.66	81.82
Crotch (CL-2CD)	15.7	16.36	17.02	17.68	18.34	19	19.66	20.32

BASIC GRADING FOR WOVEN GARMENTS

On the previous page, measurements for US sizes 0-14 are equivalent to UK sizes 4-18. Number sizes increase in circumference by 2" or 5 cm. The basic grade rule for each number size is 2" or 5 cm. Letter sizes encompass two number sizes. The grade rule from XS to S is 4" or 10 cm.

Grade rules differ for the height of a garment. The crotch depth grade is 1/2" or 12.5 mm and the crotch length is 1 1/4" or 32 mm.

BASIC GRADING FOR STRETCH GARMENTS

After the basic grade rules have been developed, a second grade rule is created for incorporating stretch. Use the reduction charts on pages 92 and 93 to create a custom chart.

The chart below is based on the width stretch measurements for the classification "Stretchy" found on page 93. The grade amount is reduced based on the stretch. The height grade is also reduced, but based on the stretch for "Moderate Stretch" for the vertical stretch of the fabric.

IMPERIAL GRADE RULES
Measurements in Inches

	Full Grade Amount		Reduced for Stretch	
	Number Size	Letter Size	Number Size	Letter Size
Waist	2	4	1.63	3.25
High Hip	2	4	1.63	3.25
Low Hip	2	4	1.63	3.25
Crotch Depth	.5	1	.43	.85
Crotch Length	1.25	2.5	1.09	2.18
Crotch (CL-2CD)	.25	.5	.23	.45

METRIC GRADE RULES
Measurements in Centimeters

	Full Grade Amount		Reduced for Stretch	
	Number Size	Letter Size	Number Size	Letter Size
Waist	5	10	4.06	8.12
High Hip	5	10	4.06	8.12
Low Hip	5	10	4.06	8.12
Crotch Depth	1.25	2.5	1.09	2.18
Crotch Length	3.18	6.35	2.77	5.54
Crotch (CL-2CD)	.64	1.25	.56	1.09

Not all designers create separate stretch grade rules. Many develop their grade based on one size and grade the standard amount, not incorporating stretch. This may not be noticeable in an XS - XL grade but can be noticeable for a larger range.

In US Sizes over XL or size 14, patterns generally have a larger grade amount, in the amount of 1.5x the normal grade. In US Sizes over a 2X or size 18, patterns may grade at 2x the normal grade.

GRADE DIVISION

The grade division is based on how the grade is split over the entire body of the garment. Since grading usually involves half of the front and half of the back, the grade needs to be divided into four parts, one for each quarter of the body.

The grade division splits the width grade by one quarter. In the tables below, the reduced stretch grade rules are split for grading one quarter of the body. The height grade is not affected by the width grade.

GRADE DIVISION - REDUCED FOR STRETCH
Measurements in Inches

	Number Size Grade Rule	Grade Division	Letter Size Grade Rule	Grade Division
Width Grade	1.63	0.41	3.25	0.81
Height Grade	.43		.85	
Crotch Grade	.23		.45	

GRADE DIVISION - REDUCED FOR STRETCH
Measurements in Centimeters

	Number Size Grade Rule	Grade Division	Letter Size Grade Rule	Grade Division
Width Grade	4.06	1.02	8.12	2.03
Height Grade	1.09		2.18	
Crotch Grade	.56		1.09	

CHAPTER 17

BOYSHORT: PATTERN DRAFTING

This chapter provides flat pattern drafting directions to create a boyshort. In addition to the basic set of instructions, variations are provided to create alternative drafts. Utilize the reduced stretch measurements for the specific fabric being used. Record the measurements taken from Chapter 16 and reduce the amounts required for the fabric stretch.

Waist Measurement			
High Hip Measurement		High Hip Depth	
Low Hip Measurement		Low Hip Depth	
Crotch Depth		Total Crotch Amount	
Front Crotch		Back Crotch	

DRAFTING BY HAND

MEASUREMENT SETUP

1. **a.** Draw a straight line, down the center of the paper.

   b. Draw a line horizontally, 2" or 5 cm up from the bottom edge of the paper.

   c. On the center vertical line, measure up the Crotch Depth and mark with a hash mark.

   d. At the bottom of the Crotch Depth, measure to the right and left 1/4 of the reduced Low Hip Measurement and mark with a hash mark.

   e. Square a line up at both ends, in the same measurement as the Crotch Depth, and mark.

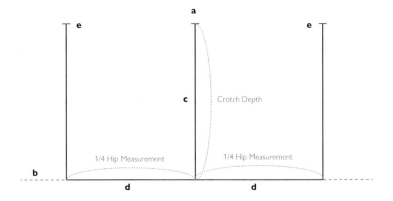

2. Label the line on the right as Center Front. Label the line on the left as Center Back. Label the center line as Side Seam. Label the bottom horizontal line as Crotch Depth.

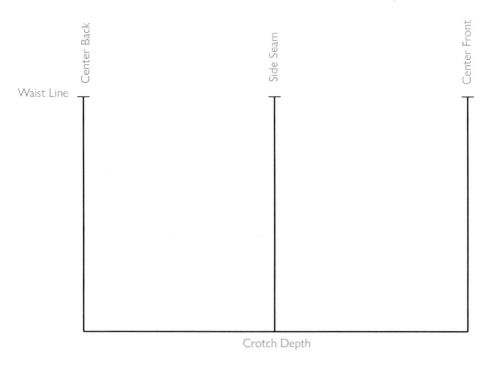

3. Divide the outside lines into two equal sections and place a hash mark in the middle.

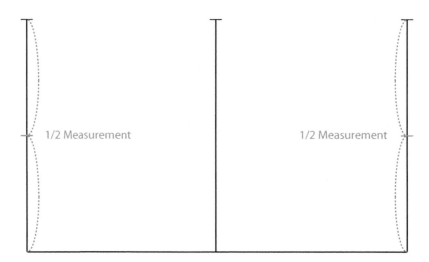

CROTCH SHAPE

4. a. Square a line to the right, at the bottom of the Center Front Line, the Front Crotch measurement.

   b. Square a line out to the left at the bottom of the Center Back Line, the Back Crotch measurement.

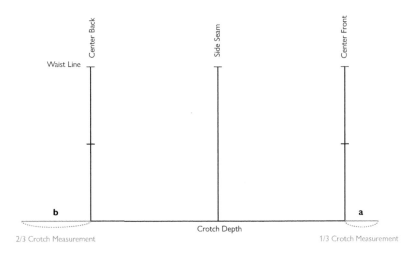

5. a. At the front crotch, take 1/2 of the Front Crotch amount and draw a 45 degree line originating at the Center Front/Crotch Depth point. The half amount creates a smooth and gradual curve for the body.

   b. At the back crotch, take 1/2 of the Back Crotch amount and draw a 45 degree line originating at the Center Back/Crotch Depth point.

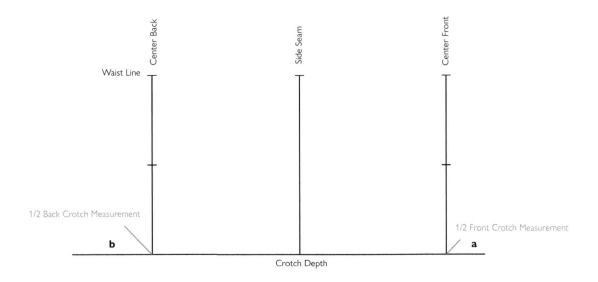

6. a. Using a curve, or series of curves, connect the front crotch point, the 45 degree line, and the center point on the Center Front.

    b. Repeat the same step on the back. If there is an unsightly point where this curve meets the Center Back line, use the curve to blend out the point as pictured.

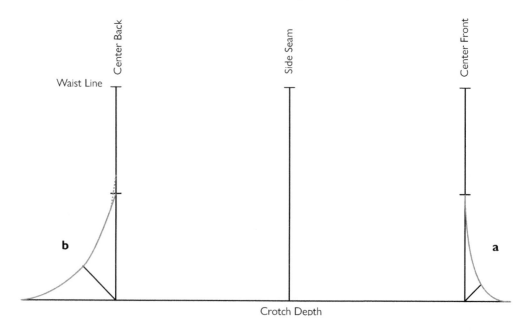

7. At the bottom of the crotch curve for both the front and back, square a line down, at 90 degrees from the last 1/4" or 6 mm of the curve. Mark the line at 1/2 of the Full Crotch Width. This amount should be between 1" or 2.5 cm and 1 1/2" or 3.8 cm.

Based on the explanation in Chapter 10, the width can vary based on skeletal structure. The amount used in pattern making is between 2" or 5 cm and 3" or 7.6 cm, averaging at 2 1/2" or 6.4 cm.

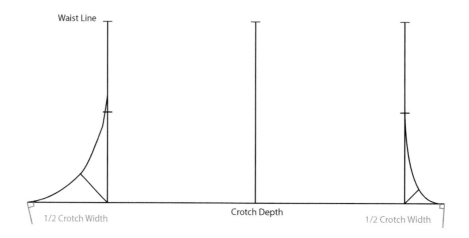

LEG OPENING

8. Raise the entire side seam, in the amount of 1/6 of the Crotch Depth. Raising this point is recommended as the body is not flat. This amount can be altered for design.

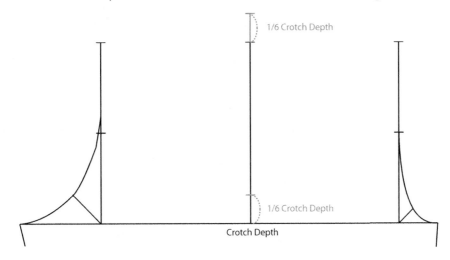

1/6 Crotch Depth

1/6 Crotch Depth

Crotch Depth

9. a. Create a front leg slope by connecting the front crotch area to the raised side seam with a straight line. Divide this line by two and mark it.

 b. Create a back leg slope by connecting the back crotch area to the raised side seam with a straight line. Divide this line by three and mark the third closest to the back crotch.

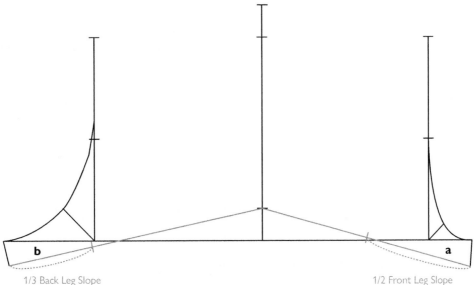

b

a

1/3 Back Leg Slope

1/2 Front Leg Slope

10. a. On the front marking (right side), square a short line up from the front leg slope line, 1/2" - 1" (12.5 mm to 25 mm) at a 90 degree angle. This amount can vary depending on the leg curvature desired.

   b. On the back marking (left side), square a short line down from the back leg slope line, 1/2" - 1" (12.5 mm or 25mm) at a 90 degree angle. This amount can vary depending on the coverage desired and the size of the garment. As garment sizes decrease, a smaller amount should be used. As sizes increase, the amount used should increase also. Recommended: XS - 1/2" or 12.5 mm, small - 5/8" or 15 mm, medium - 3/4" or 19 mm, large - 7/8" or 22 mm, XL - 1" or 25 mm.

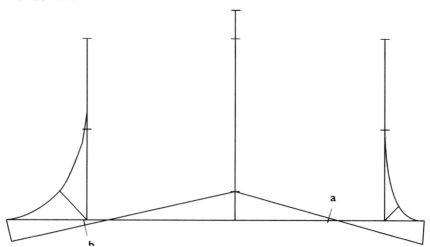

11. Use a series of curves, as pictured, to connect the back crotch, side seam, and front crotch points.

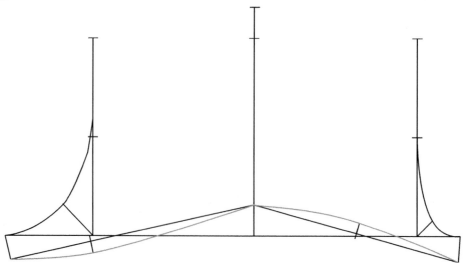

SIDE SEAM

12. a. Square a line across the top of the raised Side Seam and extend the Center Front and Center Back to meet this line. Label this as New Waist line.

  b. Find the midpoint of the new raised Side Seam or measure down from the New Waist line the High Hip Depth, and mark.

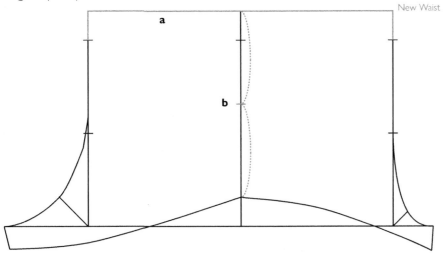

13. a. At the the point marked in step 12b, square a horizontal line across to meet both the Center Front and Center Back.

  b. On the New Waist line, from the Center Front, measure towards the Side Seam 1/4 of the Waist Measurement. Repeat for the back.

  c. On the line created in step 13a, from the Center Front, measure towards the Side Seam 1/4 of the High Hip Measurement. Repeat for the back.

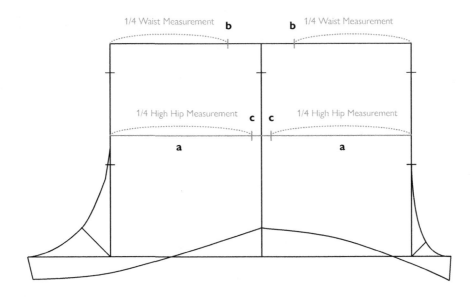

VARIATION A: HIGH WAIST BOYSHORT

14. a. At the waist line marking, measure up 1/2" or 12.5 mm to allow for the curvature of the body on the waist shape. This amount can vary based on the end user, but this is average to create curvature on the waist line. This amount can be increased or decreased for the intended customer.

    b. Using a hip curve, connect the raised 1/2" or 12.5 mm mark, the high hip marking, and the lower hip point. These points may not meet exactly, but use curved rulers to create a smooth shape for the side seam. Match the shape of the front side seam curve to the back.

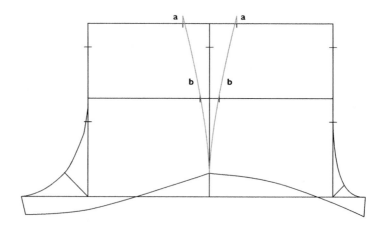

15. a. Create the back waist line shape, by connecting the Center Back to the raised side seam point with a curve.

    b. Create the front waist line shape, by connecting the Center Front to the raised side seam point with a curve.

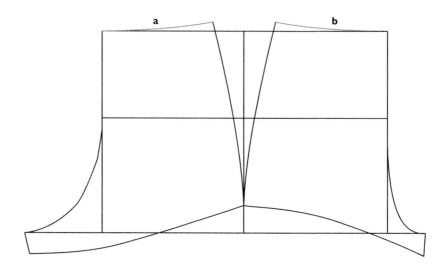

VARIATION B: ELIMINATE SIDE SEAM

Follow steps 1-13, then continue with step 14 below. Eliminating the curvature to the side seam allows the front and back to be joined as a single pattern piece.

14. a. Using a straight ruler, draw a line from the low hip point through the high hip marking, extending through the New Waist line.

    b. At the New Waist line, extend the line 1/2" or 12.5 mm.

    c. Measure the difference of the original side seam to the new side seam on the New Waist line. Move the center front and center back of the draft towards the Side Seam, in the same amount the side seam was altered.

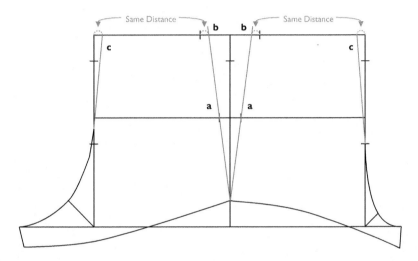

15. Create the curved waist line shape, connecting the center front of the brief to the altered side seam. Repeat for the back.

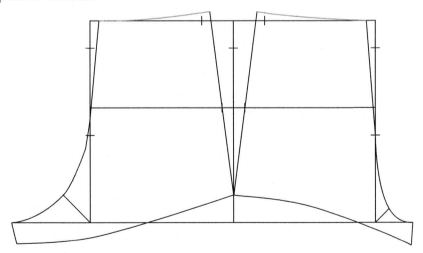

VARIATION C: HIP HUGGER

Follow steps 1-13, and step 14 of Variation A: High Waist Boyshort, then continue with the following step to create the hip hugger low rise boyshort.

15. To create a hip hugger style, the boyshort is altered to sit at the hip bone, which is near the high hip. In this example, the back is drafted to sit higher than the front. The front is drafted to the High Hip line. This design provides more coverage in the back. The side seam length for the front and back must be equal in length in order for the seams to connect properly.

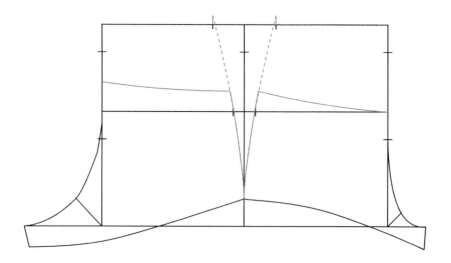

CROTCH LINING

16. Confirm that a 90 degree angle is present at the bottom of the center curve. Double check that the length of the crotch width is equal for the front and back.

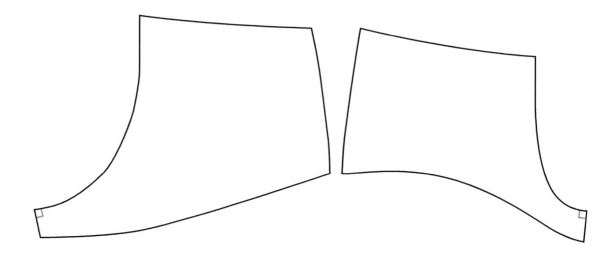

17. Place the front and back pieces end to end, joining together at the center of the crotch area. Be sure to smooth the curves from the front to back on both sides of the joined crotch pieces if they are pointed or shaped oddly.

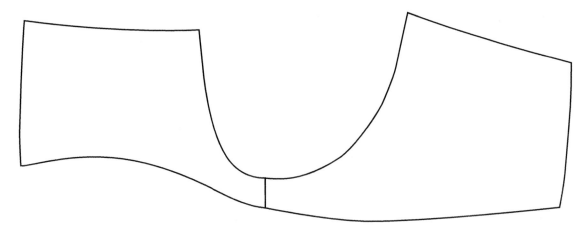

18. Determine the coverage and lining size preferred. This can vary and is only one example.

   a. On the front, starting at the joined crotch seam, measure out on the leg, towards the side seam, the front crotch amount. Square a line towards the crotch curve and measure the distance of the new line.

   b. On the back, starting at the joined crotch seam, measure out on the leg, towards the side seam, the back crotch amount. Square a line towards the crotch curve and measure the distance of the line.

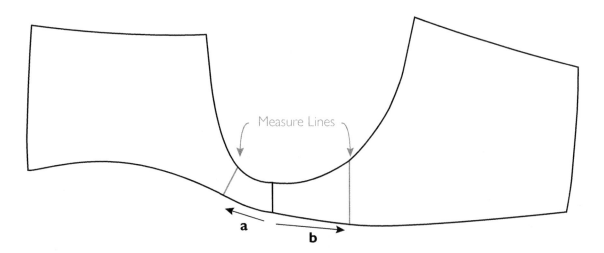

19. a. On a separate piece of paper, draw a straight horizontal line the length of the Total Crotch Amount (Front Crotch + Back Crotch).

  b. On the side of the front, square a line up in the amount measured in the previous step 18a.

  c. On the side of the back, square a line up in the amount measured in the previous step 18b.

  d. At the center crotch seam, square a line up in the amount of half the crotch width.

  e. Use a curve to create the pattern piece.

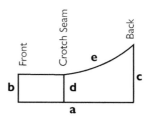

DRAFTING BY ILLUSTRATION SOFTWARE

Create a draft by hand and complete the measurement chart prior to drafting with CAD (Computer Aided Design). The pictured amounts are imperial and based on the charts in Chapter 16. Substitute these numbers with the numbers from the chart on page 99. The following draft looks similar to the hand draft, with the back on the left and the front on the right. Basic drafting can be replicated in Adobe® Illustrator®. The following steps can be modified based on design.

1. Using the *Rectangle Tool*, create a rectangle in the measurements of the Low Hip Width (Width) and the Crotch Depth (Height). This is the base of the back.

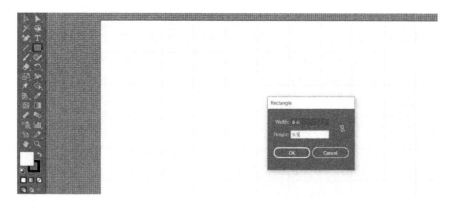

2. Using the *Rectangle Tool*, create a rectangle in the measurements of the Back Crotch (Width) and 1/2 of the Crotch Depth (Height). This is the base of the back crotch.

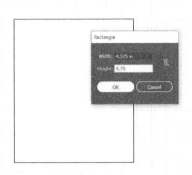

3. a. Align the second rectangle on the lower left side of the first rectangle. Duplicate the rectangle created in step 1 and align them side by side. This is the base of the front.

b. Using the *Rectangle Tool*, create a rectangle with the Front Crotch (Width) and 1/2 of the Crotch Depth (Height). Align to the lower right side. This is the base of the front crotch.

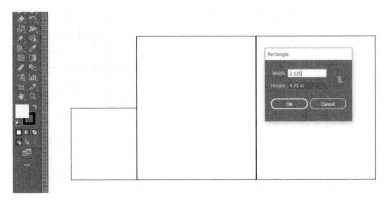

4. Use the *Line Tool* and click on the lower right intersection of the left two boxes. Enter in 1/2 of the Back Crotch (Length) with the angle of 135 degrees.

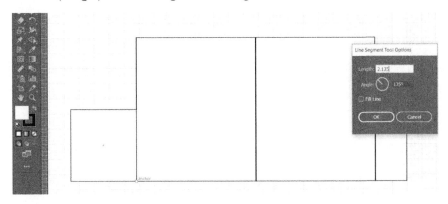

5. Use the *Line Tool* and click on the lower left intersection of the right two boxes. Enter in 1/2 of the Front Crotch (Length) with the angle of 45 degrees.

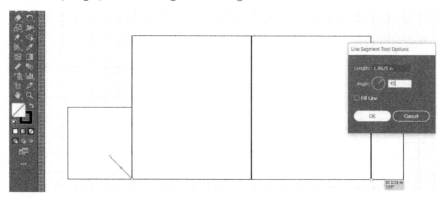

6. a. Use the *Direct Selection Tool* and select the entire center on the pattern and press Enter. This is the side seam.

    b. Use 1/6 of the Crotch Depth amount and enter that into the Vertical field, leaving the Horizontal field as 0.

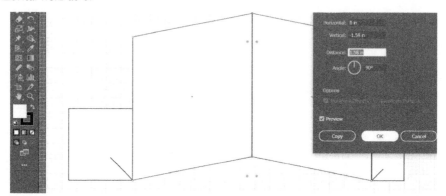

7. Using the *Pen Tool*, draw in a curve for the inseam, connecting the lower left point on the small left rectangle to the top opposite point, hitting the center diagonal line. Repeat for the front.

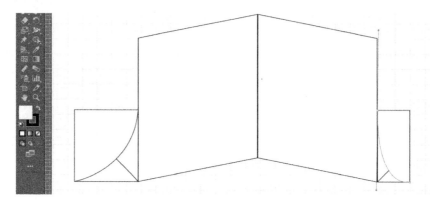

8. Using the *Line Tool*, start a line from the lower left side at a visibly 90 degree angle from the curve in the length of 1/2 the Crotch Width. Drawing the line at the exact amount is difficult. Draw a short line in the angle, delete the line, then click on the point and the angle is saved from the previous drawing. Enter in the amount of 1/2 the Crotch Width.

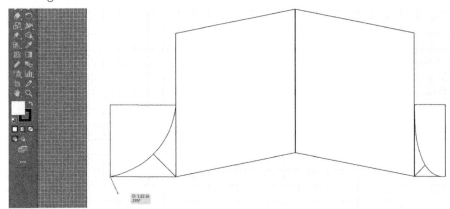

9. Repeat Step 8 on the far right side.

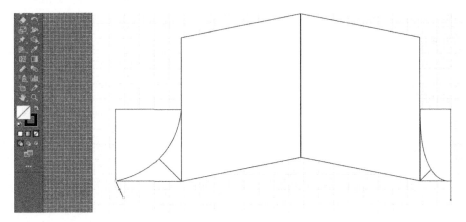

10. Using the *Pen Tool*, connect the lower left point of the curve to a point just below the angled line. This amount does not need to be exact. Draw the shape and adjust as necessary.

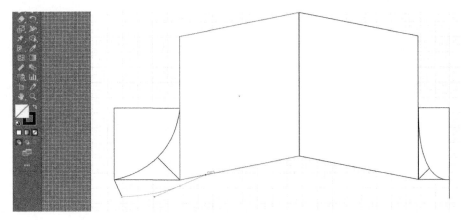

11. Continuing with the *Pen Tool*, connect to the center line.

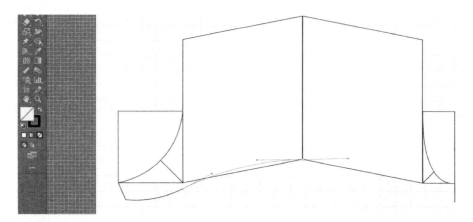

12. Continue with the *Pen Tool* and draw a line to approximately the halfway point on the right side.

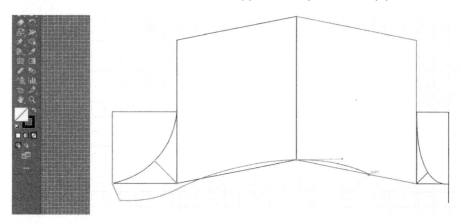

13. Complete the leg curve to the right side of the crotch width on the front.

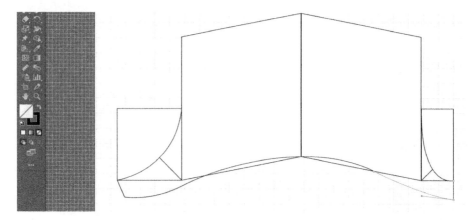

14. On the back side, use the *Pen Tool* and connect the left inseam curve, and use the guidelines in the software to line up the top of the front to the height of the side seam.

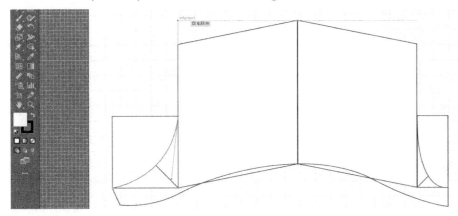

15. On the *Layers Menu*, select the front side rectangle and lock it. Using the *Direct Selection Tool*, select the far right top side of the back rectangle and press Enter. Enter in the difference of the hip measurement to the waist measurement in the Horizontal field (Hip minus Waist) and 1/2" or 12.5 mm in the Vertical field for adding curvature to the waist line. Unlock the front and repeat the same step, for the front, in the opposite direction.

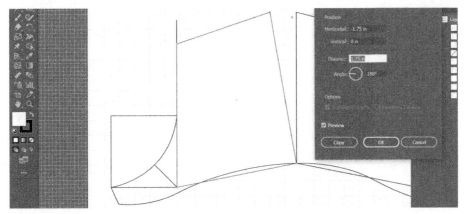

16. Using the *Pen Tool*, connect the top of the back to the side of the altered side seam of the back.

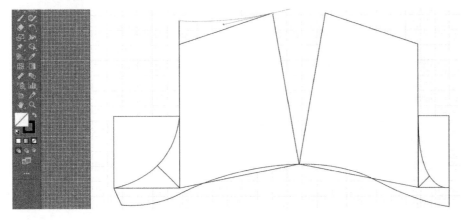

17. Complete the back portion by drawing in the side seam with a curve.

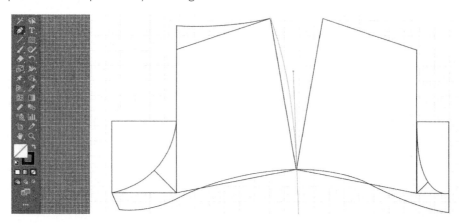

18. Repeat the steps on the front side of the boyshort. Use the *Cutting Tool* to separate the leg curve at the side seam.

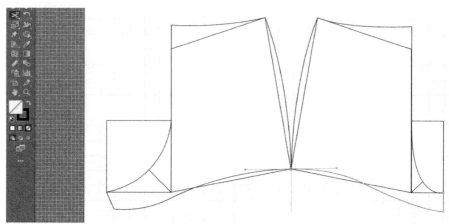

19. Select the body and the leg curve of the corresponding side, select *Object* -> *Path* -> *Join* to create independent front and back pieces.

CHAPTER 18

BOYSHORT: GRADING

Record the grade amounts from Chapter 16. Generally, most panties are graded using letter size grade rules, XS-XL. Both number and letter size grade rules are listed in the below chart. Divide the Grade Rule by four, as instructed in Chapter 16, to determine the Grade Division below. The Grade Division is considered the Full Grade amount on the following pages.

	Number Size Grade Rule	Grade Division	Letter Size Grade Rule	Grade Division
Width Grade				
Height Grade				
Crotch Grade				

GRADING BY HAND

1. **a.** Draw a horizontal line on paper. This line intersects the bottom of the crotch curve.

   b. Draw a vertical line several inches from the right and left edges of the paper.

   c. Trace the half draft of both the front and back. Be sure to exclude any seam allowances that may have been added during the testing process. Line up the top point of the crotch width to the horizontal line and the center front and center back to the vertical lines.

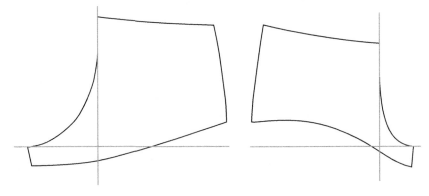

GRADING GUIDELINES

2. The height of the panty is graded using horizontal grading guidelines.

    a. On the horizontal line drawn in the previous step, label as the 0 Grade.

    b. Place a horizontal line where the waistline sat from the draft. This is the Full Height Grade.

    c. Divide the remainder of the body into 3 equal parts. Each of these lines represents a proportion of the body.

    d. The second line down represents the high hip and the 2/3 Height Grade.

    e. The third line down represents the low hip and the 1/3 Height Grade.

Visually refer to all drafting and grading as following a proportion of the body. If drafting a garment that is 2/3 the height of a full coverage garment, use 2/3 of the full height grade amount.

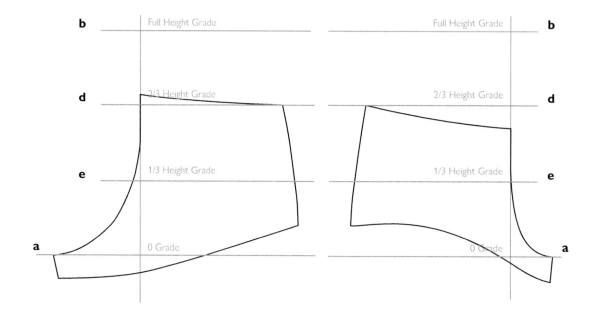

3. The width of the panty is graded using vertical grading guidelines.

   a. On the vertical guides drawn at the center front and center back, label this as the 0 Grade.

   b. Place a vertical line at the outside point of the side seam. Mark this as the Full Width Grade.

   c. Divide the space between the 0 Grade and the Full Width Grade into 3 equal parts.

   d. The second line from the Full Width Grade is the 2/3 Width Grade.

   e. The third line is the 1/3 Width Grade.

   f. The Crotch Grade is slightly different and is based on how the crotch amount is split in Chapter 16. The front crotch represents 1/3 of the Crotch Grade.

   g. The back crotch represents 2/3 of the Crotch Grade.

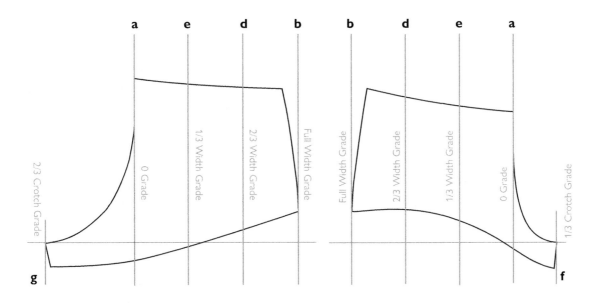

GRADE SPLIT

4. Refer to the size chart at the beginning of the chapter for the grading rules. The Grade Division is used as the Full Grade amount below. Fill out the grade split below based on the size range being graded. Divide the Full Grade amount for the width, height, and crotch into three parts and complete the chart below.

REDUCED GRADE SPLIT CHART

	Grade Division/ Full Grade	2/3 Grade	1/3 Grade
Width Grade			
Height Grade			
Crotch Grade			

ADDITIONAL GUIDELINES

5. a. Draw a perpendicular line, from the 2/3 Horizontal Grade line, at the waist side seam point, parallel to the Center Front and Back.

   b. Draw a perpendicular line, from the 1/3 Horizontal Grade line, at the side seam/leg point, parallel to the Center Front and Back.

   c. Draw a horizontal line, from the 0 Vertical Grade, at the lower crotch point, perpendicular to the Center Front and Back.

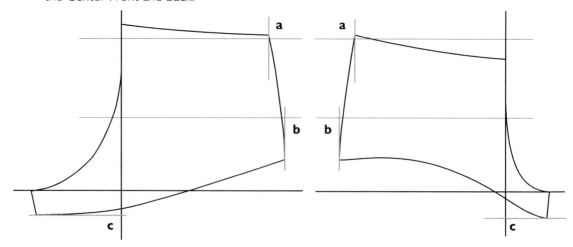

WAIST/SIDE SEAM GRADE

In the following steps, the base size is graded down one size. According to the grade guidelines, the height change, for this boyshort, sits at the 2/3 Height Grade line. Alter the grade amounts based on where your boyshort draft sits on the body.

6. a. Height Grade – At the center front, center back, and tops of the side seam, decrease the height on the vertical lines by the 2/3 Height Grade amount.

   b. Width Grade – At the top of the new height grade of the side seams, grade inward the Full Width Grade.

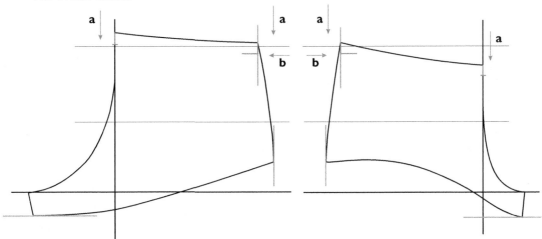

CROTCH GRADE

7. a. Front Crotch Grade – Mark inward a parallel line to the existing crotch seam, 1/3 of the Crotch Grade.

   b. Back Crotch Grade – Mark inward a parallel line to the existing crotch seam, 2/3 of the Crotch Grade.

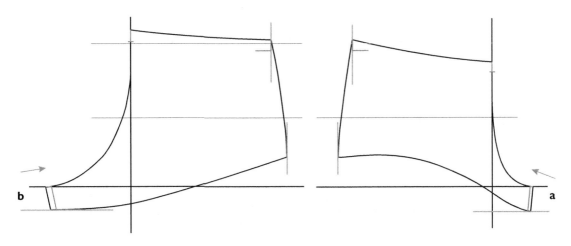

LEG/SIDE SEAM GRADE

8. a. Height Grade – The bottom of the side seam sits between the 0 Grade and the 1/3 Grade position. This position can be graded at half of the 1/3 Grade amount. Some designers do not grade this position at all for height. Measure down on the guideline 1/6 of the height grade.

   b. Width Grade – Measure inward the Full Grade amount, making it perpendicular to the guideline.

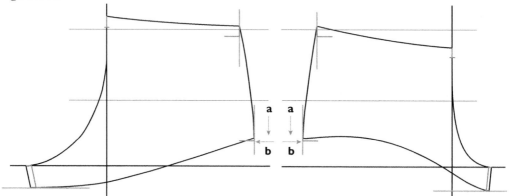

9. Draw in the new size, connecting each new grade point. Repeat for each additional size required.

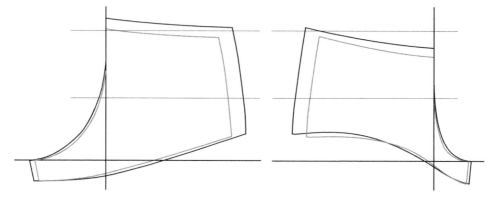

10. The lining will vary in grade amounts based on the narrowing or widening of the pattern in the curve of the crotch. To properly grade the lining, follow steps 18 and 19 from the previous chapter to determine the changes required for lining.

   a. Front Crotch Grade – Mark inward a parallel line to the existing crotch seam, 1/3 of the Crotch Grade.

   b. Back Crotch Grade – Mark inward a parallel line to the existing crotch seam, 2/3 of the Crotch Grade.

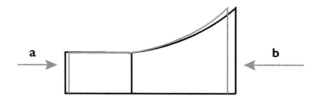

GRADING BY ILLUSTRATION SOFTWARE

Utilize the grade chart on page 120 for custom grade amounts. This example uses the imperial chart amounts from Chapter 16. Recreate this grade using the custom amounts for the stretch and size grade previously determined.

1. Label the grade amounts in Adobe® Illustrator® based on the chart. Copy each pattern piece and lock one set in the *Layers Menu*.

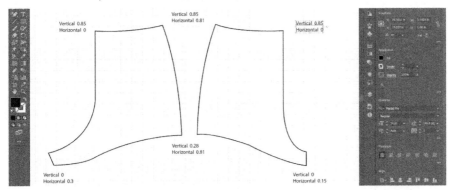

2. Using the *Direct Selection Tool*, select the center waistline corner of the back and press enter. Enter the grade amounts. Based on how Adobe® Illustrator® is set up, movements up and to the left generally use negative values.

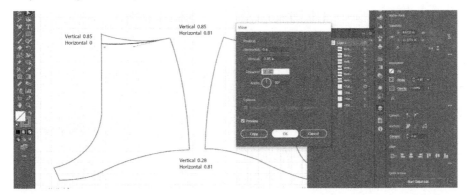

3. Using the *Direct Selection Tool*, select the side seam waistline corner of the back and press enter. Enter the grade amounts into the dialog box.

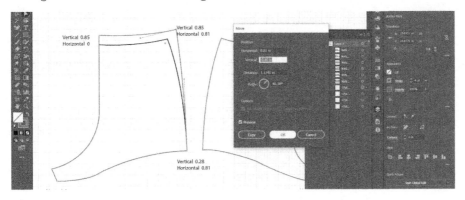

4. Select the lower side seam of the back and press enter. Enter the grade amounts.

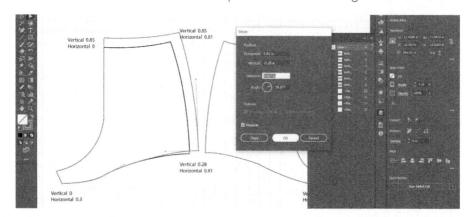

5. Select the entire crotch width line and press enter. Enter the grade amounts.

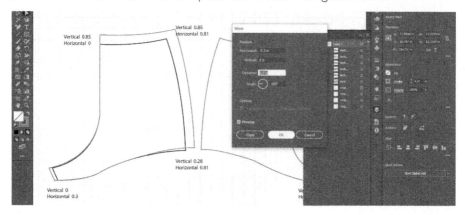

6. Repeat the steps for the front grade. Follow these steps for each size in the desired size range.

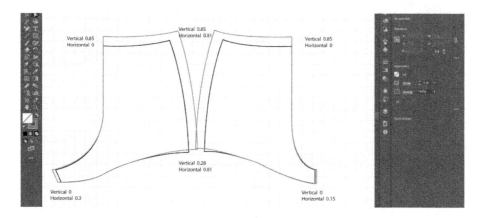

CHAPTER 19

BRIEF: PATTERN DRAFTING

This chapter demonstrates how to pattern draft a brief. Variations are provided for altering the waistline and leg shapes. Instructions for a thong draft follow the basic brief directions under the Drafting by Hand section. Utilize the measurements taken in Chapter 16, reduce based on the stretch, and record below for easy reference.

Waist Measurement			
High Hip Measurement		High Hip Depth	
Low Hip Measurement		Low Hip Depth	
Crotch Length		Crotch Depth	
Front Crotch		Back Crotch	

DRAFTING BY HAND

MEASUREMENT SETUP

1. a. Leaving approximately 2" or 5 cm at the top of the paper and 8" or 20 cm at the bottom, draw a straight line down the center in the amount of the Crotch Depth.

   b. At each end of the Crotch Depth line, draw a line to both the right and left, 1/4 of the Low Hip Measurement.

   c. Square lines down at both ends of the 1/4 Low Hip Measurement to create two rectangles.

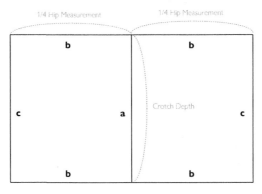

2. a. Divide the center vertical line into three equal sections or utilize the High Hip and Low Hip depth for a custom draft. The first third down equates to the High Hip Depth and the second third down equates to the Low Hip Depth.

  b. Square lines across at each of these markings.

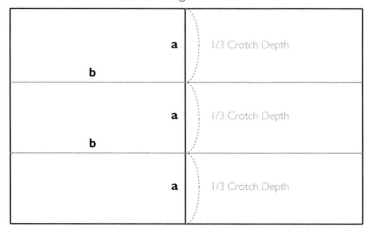

3. Label the lines as pictured: Center Back, Side Seam, Center Front, Waist, High Hip, Low Hip, and Crotch Depth.

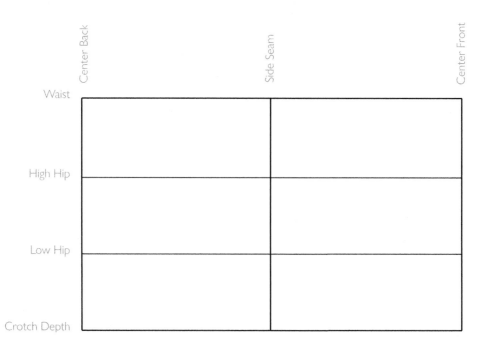

CROTCH SHAPE

4. a. Extend the Center Front line down in the amount of the Front Crotch Measurement (which is 1/3 of the total crotch amount calculated on page 94).

  b. Extend the Center Back line down in the amount of the Back Crotch Measurement (which is 2/3 of the total crotch amount calculated on page 94). Place a mark indicating the center of this line.

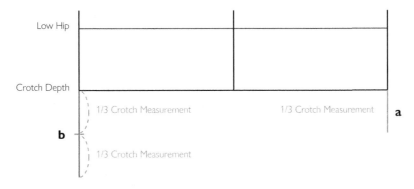

5. a. At the bottom of the crotch measurement for both the Front and Back, square a line across, towards the Side Seam, 1/2 of the Full Crotch Width. This amount should be between 1" or 2.5 cm and 1 1/2" or 3.8 cm, based on anatomy and preference. Refer to Chapter 10.

  b. On the front side of the Crotch Depth line, measure towards the Side Seam, half the Crotch Width measurement plus 1/8" or 3mm. This amount can vary based on preference.

  c. At the center marking on the Back Crotch, square across the width chosen as the Crotch Width.

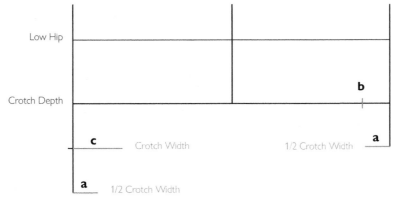

6. a. On the front side, use a curve to connect the point on the Crotch Depth line to the half crotch width.

b. On the back side, use a curve to connect the two lower crotch lines.

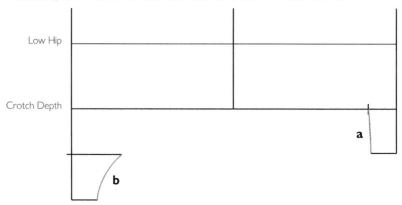

VARIATION A: HIGH WAIST BRIEF

A full draft goes up to the waistline. This draft is best used to create a sloper as it covers more of the body.

WAISTLINE

7. a. At the Waist line, for both the front and back, measure towards the Side Seam, 1/4 of the Waist Measurement and mark.

b. At the new side seam/waist marking, measure up 1/2" or 12.5 mm. This 1/2" or 12.5 mm helps account for the curvature of the body. This amount can be increased or decreased for the intended customer or for preference.

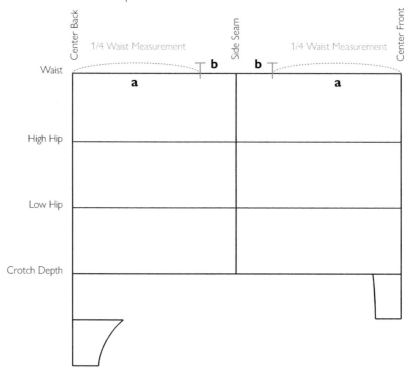

8. Use a hip curve to connect the waist point, at the Center Front and Center Back, to the 1/2" or 12.5 mm markings at the side seam of the draft. Be sure that this curve is not too extreme, or it may not sew together well.

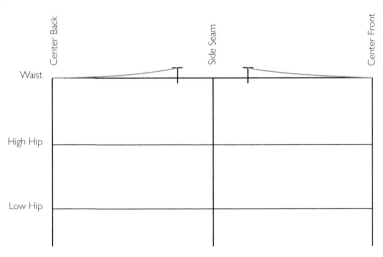

SIDE SEAM

9. **a.** At the High Hip line, at the Center Front and Center Back, measure towards the Side Seam 1/4 of the High Hip Measurement and mark.

   b. On the Side Seam, mark the halfway point between the Low Hip line and the Crotch Depth. This equals 1/6 of the Crotch Depth. This marking is to indicate where the lowest point of the brief will sit on the leg. This point sits level to the crotch when worn.

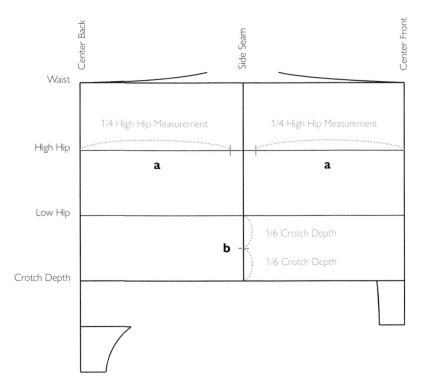

10. Using a hip curve, connect the waistline, the high hip marking, and the lowered hip point. These points may not meet exactly. Use these points as a guide, in order to create the side seam curve.

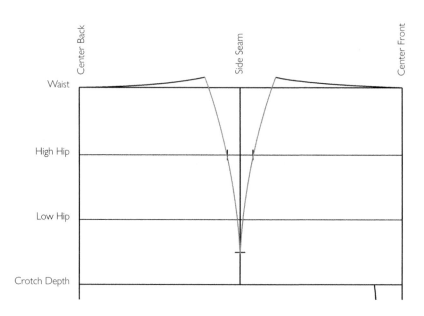

LEG OPENING

11. a. Create a front leg slope by drawing a straight line from the front crotch shape to the low hip point on the Side Seam. Divide the line by three and mark the first third toward the crotch.

    b. Create a back leg slope by drawing a straight line from the back crotch shape to the low hip point on the Side Seam. Divide the line by two and mark the center.

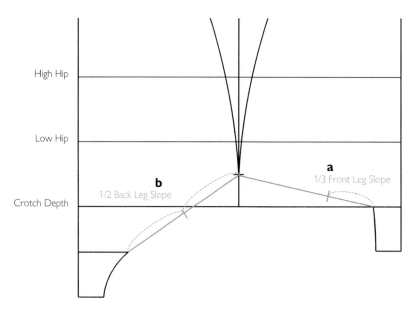

12. a. On the front marking measure up, in a 90 degree angle from the front leg slope, 1/2" to 1 1/2" (12.5 mm to 38 mm). Recommendations: XS - 1/2" or 12.5 mm, small - 3/4" or 19 mm, medium - 1" or 25 mm, large - 1 1/4" or 32 mm, XL - 1 1/2" or 38 mm.

   b. On the back marking measure down, in a 90 degree angle from the back leg slope, 1/2" to 1" (12.5 mm to 25 mm). Recommendations: XS - 1/2" or 12.5 mm, small - 5/8" or 15 mm, medium - 3/4" or 19 mm, large - 7/8" or 22 mm, XL - 1" or 25 mm.

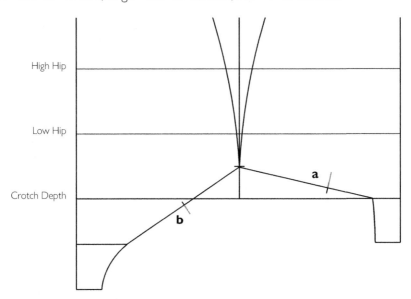

13. a. On the front leg, use a hip curve to connect the crotch point, the 1/3 marking, and the Side Seam.

   b. On the back leg, use a hip curve to connect the crotch point, the 1/2 marking, and the Side Seam. The curve will need to be flipped halfway through, in order to achieve this shape.

   c. Use a curve to create a smooth transition from the front to the back.

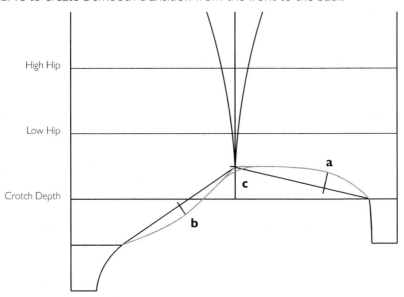

VARIATION B: HIP HUGGER BRIEF

In order to complete the following draft, complete steps 1-6 for the basic brief. The following steps create a hip hugger, high cut brief. This style drops the waistline to the high hip level on the body.

WAISTLINE

7. a. From the Center Front and Center Back, mark 1/4 of the High Hip Measurement on the High Hip line.

    b. This draft alters the position of the waistline with a lower slope at the front. The front waistline is dropped twice the back waistline amount. This can be altered for preference or design.

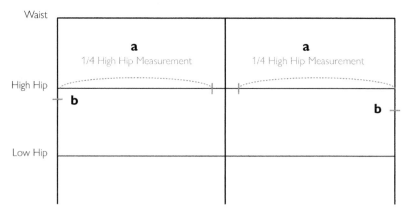

8. Use a hip curve to create the new waistline shape on both the front and back.

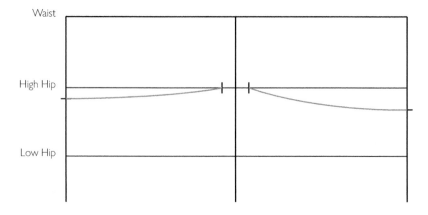

9. On the Side Seam, mark the halfway point between the Low Hip line and the Crotch Depth. This equals 1/6 of the Crotch Depth. This marking is to indicate the crotch level on the brief when worn.

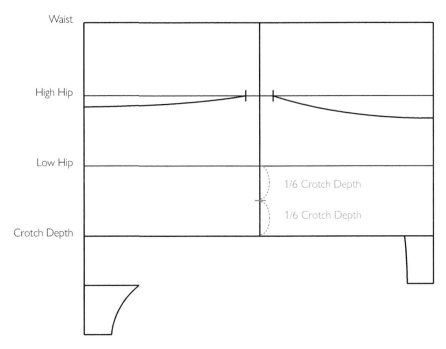

10. Using a hip curve, create a temporary side seam connecting the new waistline and the lowered hip marking for both the front and back.

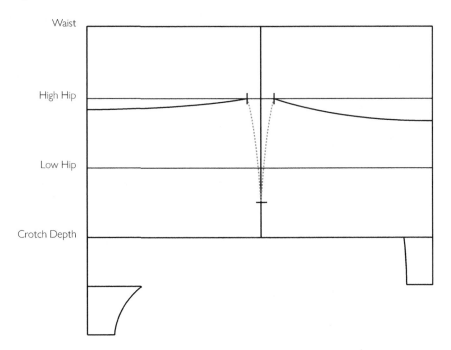

11. Determine the length desired for the side seam of the thong and mark it on the temporary side seam. Be sure to mark the front and back equally.

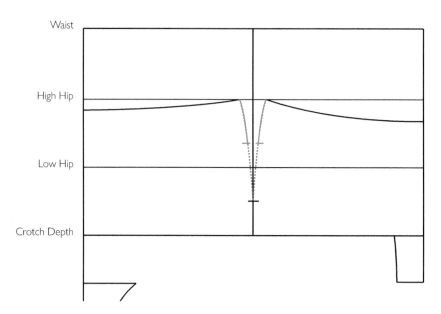

LEG OPENING

12. a. To create a front leg slope, draw a straight line from the front crotch shape to the bottom of the side seam. Divide the measurement of this slope by three and mark the first third toward the crotch.

b. To create a back leg slope, draw a straight line from the back crotch shape to the bottom of the side seam. Divide the measurement of this slope by two and mark the halfway point.

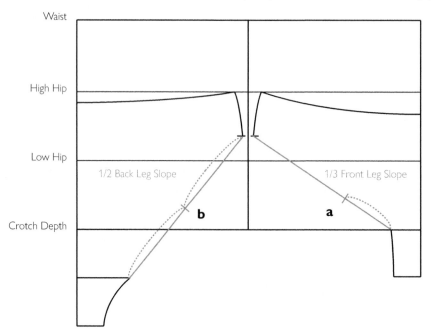

13. a. On the front marking measure up, in a 90 degree angle from the front leg slope, 1/4" to 3/4" (6 mm to 19 mm). Recommendations: XS - 1/4" or 6 mm, small - 3/8" or 10 mm, medium - 1/2" or 12.5 mm, large - 5/8" or 15 mm, XL - 3/4" or 19 mm.

   b. On the back marking measure down, in a 90 degree angle from the back leg slope, 1/2" to 1" (12.5 mm to 25 mm). Recommendations: XS - 1/2" or 12.5 mm, small - 5/8" or 15 mm, medium - 3/4" or 19 mm, large - 7/8" or 22 mm, XL - 1" or 25 mm.

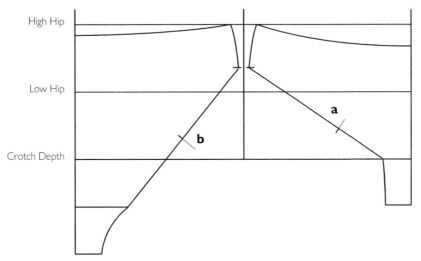

14. a. On the front leg, use a hip curve to connect the crotch point, the 1/3 marking, and the side seam.

   b. On the back leg, use a hip curve to connect the crotch point, the 1/2 marking, and the side seam. The curve will need to be flipped halfway through, in order to achieve the pictured shaping.

   c. Use a hip curve and create a smooth shape from front to back. The paper can be folded, on the side seam of the actual brief, to make this easier. Be sure that the side seams are equal.

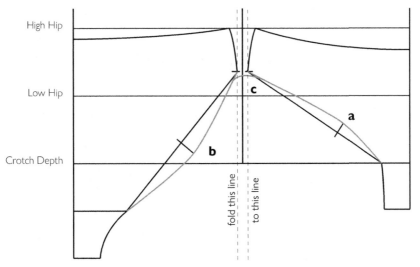

VARIATION C: THONG

These steps illustrate the drafting directions for a thong panty. Use the basic brief drafting steps 1-4, then complete these steps. This draft is designed with a high waist.

CROTCH SHAPE

5. A thong does not sit in the same position on the body that a brief sits. The crotch area of the back needs to be shortened. Divide the back crotch by three and mark each third. This amount can be adjusted for fit and comfort.

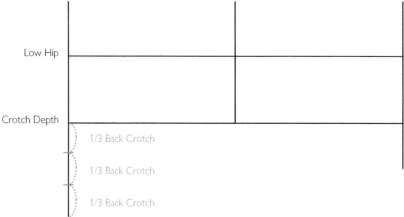

6. a. At the bottom of the front crotch, square a line towards the Side Seam, in the amount of 1/2 the Crotch Width. This amount should be between 1" or 2.5 cm and 1 1/2" or 3.8 cm. Refer to Chapter 10.

    b. At the second marking on the back, square a line towards the Side Seam 1/2 of the Crotch Width.

    c. On the front Crotch Depth line, measure towards the Side Seam, the amount of 1/2 the full Crotch Width plus 1/8" or 3 mm.

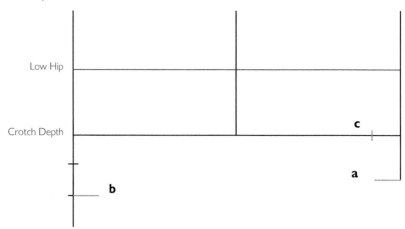

7. Using a curve, connect the front crotch to the point on the Crotch Depth line.

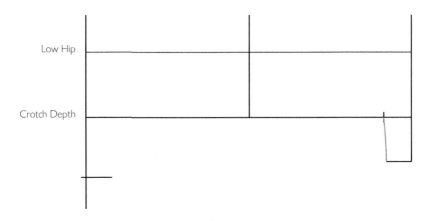

WAISTLINE

8. **a.** From the Center Front and Center Back on the Waist line, measure towards the Side Seam 1/4 of the Waist Measurement.

   b. From the Center Front and Center Back at the High Hip line, measure towards the Side Seam 1/4 of the High Hip Measurement.

   c. Divide the area between the Low Hip and the Crotch Depth in half (1/6 of the Crotch Depth).

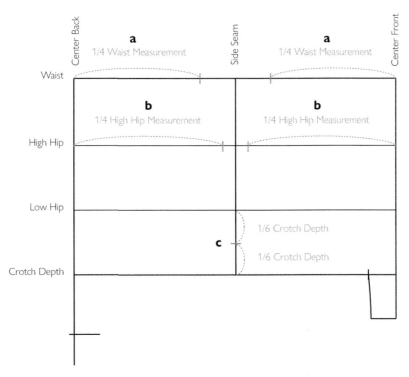

9. Use a hip curve to draw in a temporary side seam connecting the waist, high hip, and lowered hip markings for both the front and back.

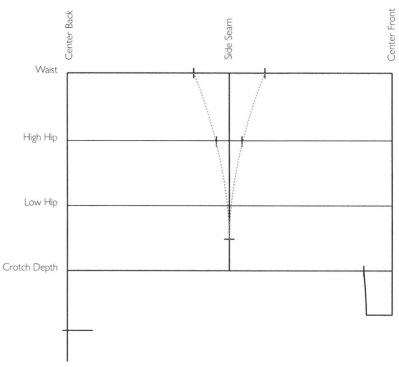

10. Mark the waistline of the front and back to design preference. To ensure curvature around the body, the side seam of the brief should sit at least 1/2" or 12.5 mm higher than the center waist. Mark the side seam. Be sure the placement on the side seam is at the exact same point for both the front and back.

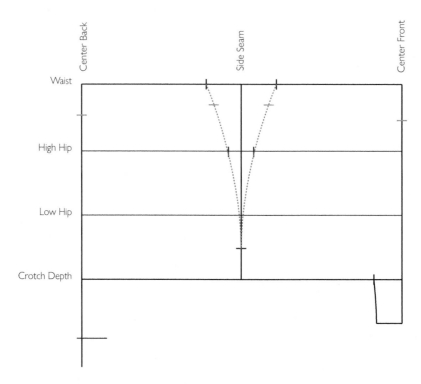

11. a. Draw in the waistline for the front and back.

    b. Choose the side seam length and draw in the side seam on the temporary side seam.

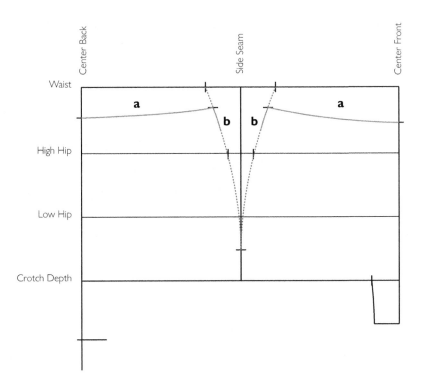

LEG OPENING

12. Create the front and back curves, based on preference. Connect the back curve to the raised crotch amount.

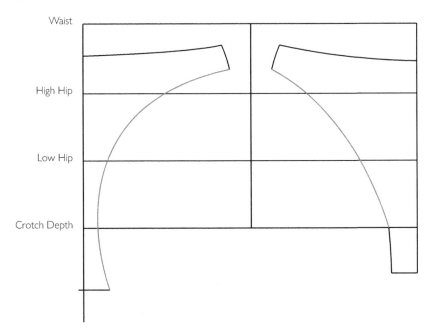

LINING

Follow these steps for all variations.

14. Line up the front and back pattern pieces for the brief at the crotch seam. At the crotch line on the front, draw a new parallel line approximately 1" or 25 mm towards the top of the front. This provides extra coverage for the lining. This amount can vary based on preference.

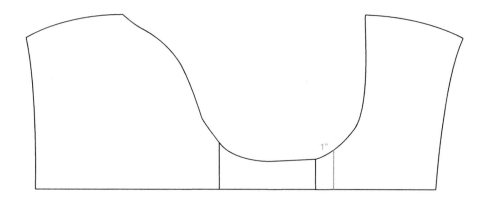

15. The area from the back crotch line with the 1" or 25 mm line becomes the lining. Separate the three pattern pieces and create a pattern to test the fit.

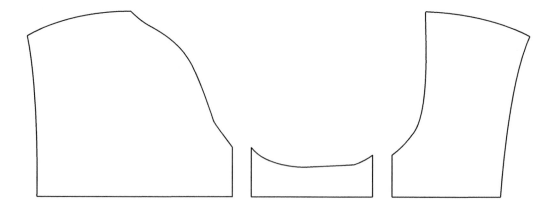

DRAFTING BY ILLUSTRATION SOFTWARE

Create a draft by hand and complete the measurement chart prior to drafting with CAD (Computer Aided Design). The pictured amounts are imperial and based on the charts in Chapter 16. Substitute these numbers with the numbers from the chart on page 125. The following draft looks similar to the hand draft, with the back on the left and the front on the right. Basic drafting can be replicated in Adobe® Illustrator®. The following steps can be modified based on design.

1. Using the *Rectangle Tool,* create a rectangle in the width of the Low Hip and the height of the Crotch Depth. This is the base of the back.

2. Using the *Rectangle Tool,* create a rectangle in the width of the Crotch Width and the length of the Back Crotch. Align the new rectangle to the lower left side of the first rectangle. This is the base of the back crotch.

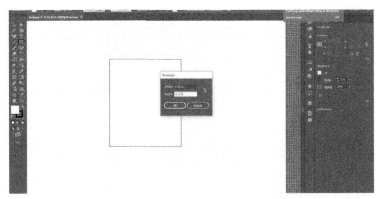

3. a. Repeat the first step and move directly next to the first rectangle to the right side. This is the base of the front.

b. Using the *Rectangle Tool,* create a rectangle in the width of the Crotch Width and the length of the Front Crotch. Align the new rectangle to the lower right side. This is the base of the front crotch.

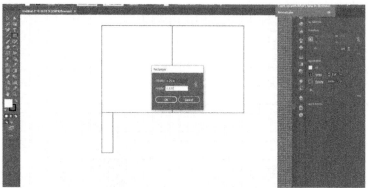

4. Copy the rectangle that was created for the front and place it next to the back crotch as pictured below.

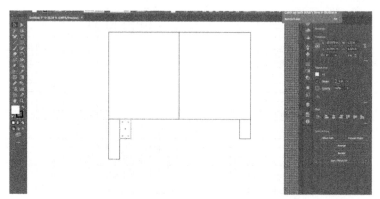

5. Lock the front rectangle. Using the *Direction Selection Tool,* select the top of the center connecting line and press enter. In the horizontal field, enter the difference between the Low Hip measurement and the Waist measurement (Low Hip minus Waist). Enter 1/2" or 12.5 mm for the vertical amount. In Adobe® Illustrator®, negative numbers are typically used to move to the position to the left or to move upwards. For the back, both numbers are negative.

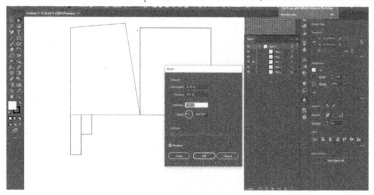

6. Unlock the front rectangle and repeat Step 5 for the front. Use a negative number for the vertical change, but a positive number for the horizontal change.

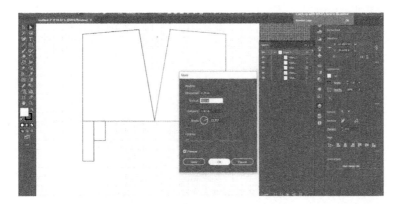

7. Using the *Direct Selection Tool,* raise the lower side seam points on both the front and back. Enter in 1/6 of the Crotch Depth in the vertical field.

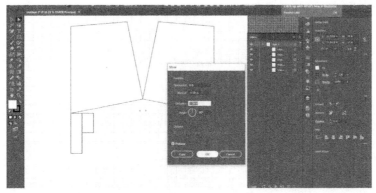

8. With the *Pen Tool,* draw in the entire back brief shape as pictured, using the modified rectangles as a guide.

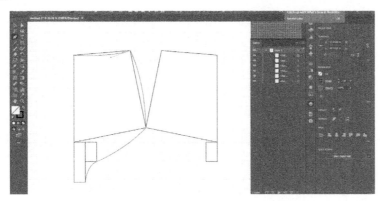

9. With the *Pen Tool*, draw in the entire front brief shape as pictured, using the modified rectangles as a guide.

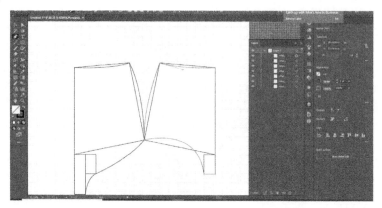

10. Adjust the back leg shape at the hip level to create a smooth shape from front to back.

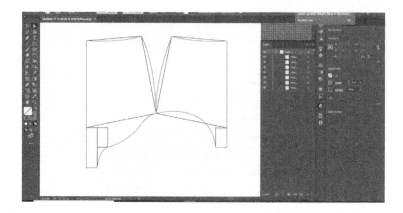

CHAPTER 20

BRIEF: GRADING

Record the grade amounts created in Chapter 16. Generally speaking, most panty designs are graded using letter size grade rules, XS-XL. Both number and letter size grade rules are shown in the below chart to accommodate everyone. Divide the Width Grade Rule by four to create the Grade Division, as instructed in Chapter 16. The Grade Division is considered the Full Grade amount on the following pages.

	Number Size Grade Rule	Grade Division	Letter Size Grade Rule	Grade Division
Width Grade				
Height Grade				
Crotch Grade				

GRADING BY HAND

1. a. Draw a horizontal line across the lower half of the pattern paper.

   b. Draw a vertical line several inches from the right and left edges of the paper.

   c. Trace the half draft of both the front and back as pictured. Be sure to exclude any seam allowances that may have been added during the testing process. Line up the top point of the Crotch Depth line to the horizontal line. Align the Center Front and Center Back to the vertical lines.

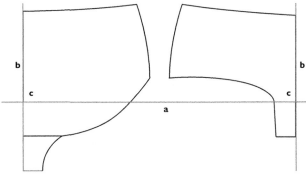

HORIZONTAL GRADING GUIDELINES

2. a. The horizontal guide created in Step 1 represents a 0 Grade.

b. Place a horizontal guide at the original waistline of the draft grid. This is the Full Height Grade.

c. Divide the space between the 0 Grade and the Full Height Grade, into three equal parts. Each division represents a different proportion of the body.

d. The line down from the Full Height Grade is the 2/3 Height Grade, also known as the High Hip.

e. The third line is the 1/3 Height Grade, also known as the Low Hip.

f. The crotch grades are slightly different and are based on how the crotch amount is initially split. Add a horizontal guide at the bottom of the front crotch. This is the 1/3 Crotch Grade

g. Draw a horizontal guide at the bottom of the back crotch. This is the 2/3 Crotch Grade.

h. Draw a horizontal guide at the middle line on the back crotch. This line is the 1/3 Crotch Grade.

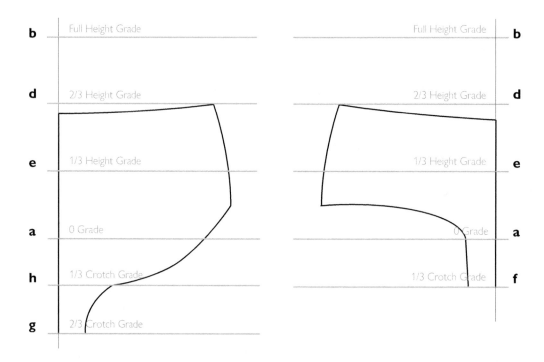

VERTICAL GRADING GUIDELINES

3. a. The vertical guides created in Step 1 indicate a 0 Grade.

   b. Place a guide for the side seam. This is the Full Width Grade.

   c. Divide the space between the 0 Grade and the Full Width Grade into 3 equal sections.

   d. The second line from the Full Width Grade is the 2/3 Width Grade.

   e. The third line is the 1/3 Width Grade.

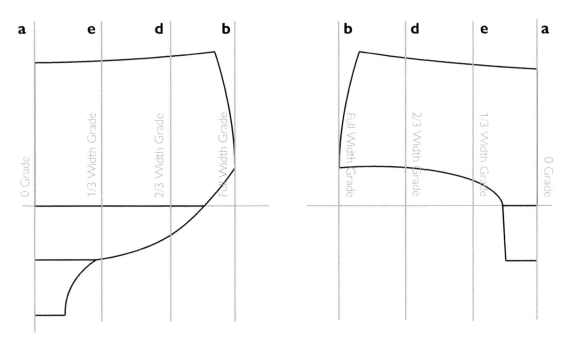

GRADE SPLIT

4. Refer to the grade chart at the beginning of the chapter. The Grade Division is used as the Full Grade amount below. Fill out the grade split below based on the size range being graded. Divide the Full Grade amount, for the width, height and crotch, by three and complete the chart below.

REDUCED GRADE SPLIT CHART			
	Grade Division/ Full Grade	2/3 Grade	1/3 Grade
Width Grade			
Height Grade			
Crotch Grade			

ADDITIONAL GUIDELINES

5. **a.** Draw a line at the waist side seam points, perpendicular to the horizintal guides, for the front and back.

   b. Draw a line at the bottom of the side seam points, perpendicular to the horizontal guides, for the front and back.

   c. Draw a line parallel to the Center Back at the higher crotch point.

   d. Draw a line parallel to the Center Back and Center Front, at the lower crotch points.

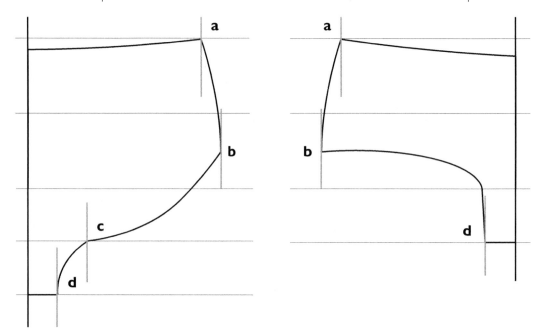

WAIST/SIDE SEAM GRADE

6. The height change falls at the 2/3 Height Grade, based on this particular style. The width uses the Full Grade amount. In this example, the grade is reduced by one size. Alter the grade amounts based on where your brief draft sits on the body.

    a. Height Grade – At the waistline, decrease the center front, center back, and side seams by the 2/3 Height Grade.

    b. Width Grade – At the side seam, measure perpendicular from the guide line the amount for the Full Width Grade.

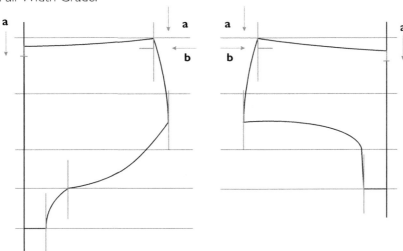

CROTCH GRADE

7. **a. Front Grade** – Raise the bottom of the front crotch up by the 1/3 Crotch Grade amount.

    b. Back Grade – Raise the upper back crotch up by the 1/3 Crotch Grade amount. Raise the bottom of the crotch up by 2/3 of the Crotch Grade amount.

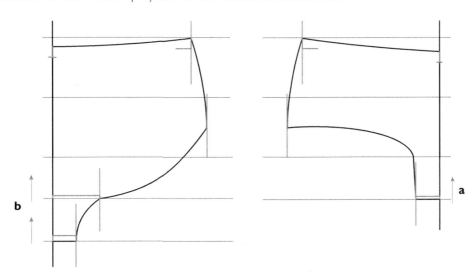

LEG/SIDE SEAM GRADE

8. a. Height Grade – The height of the lower side seam falls halfway between the 1/3 and 2/3 Grades. The grade amount falls between these two amounts, but can be altered based on design preference. Measure down, on the guideline, 1/6 of the Height Grade.

    b. Width Grade – The leg/side seam decreases by the Full Width Grade. Draw a perpendicular marking to the guideline, from the height grade.

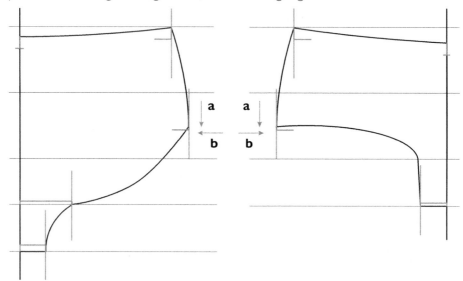

9. Draw in the sizes using curved and straight rulers. Grade each size in the desired size range.

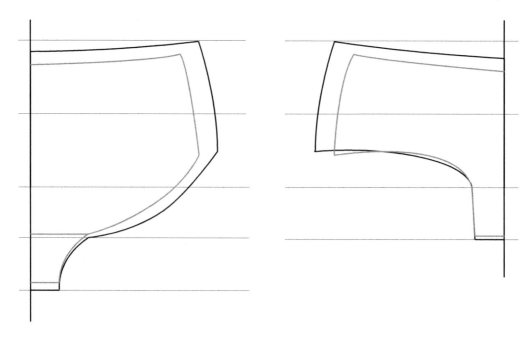

GRADING BY ILLUSTRATION SOFTWARE

Utilize the grade chart on page 147 for custom grade amounts. This example uses the imperial chart amounts from Chapter 16. Recreate this grade using the custom amounts for the stretch and size grade previously determined.

1. Label the grade amounts in Adobe® Illustrator® based on the Grade Division chart. Copy each pattern piece and lock one set in the *Layers Menu*.

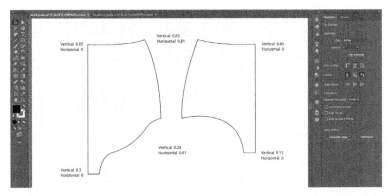

2. Use the *Direct Selection Tool* and select the top of the center back. Press enter and fill in the grade amounts. Traditionally, in Adobe® Illustrator®, negative numbers are used to move points up or to the left.

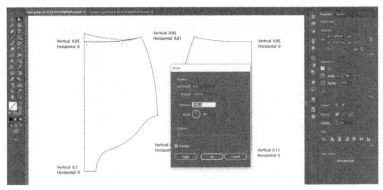

3. Using the *Direct Selection Tool*, select the waistline/side seam point of the back and enter in the grade amounts.

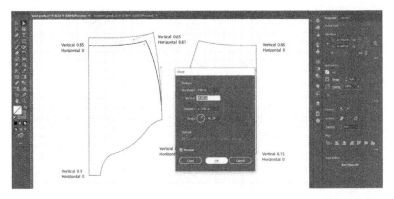

4. Use the *Direct Selection Tool* and grade the lower side seam. The two additional points on the leg may need to be slightly altered for shaping. These points can be graded in the same manner, but use smaller portions of the grade as the points are closer to the center back. Refer to the grade charts in this chapter.

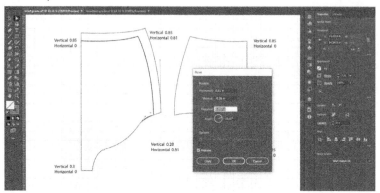

5. Grade the back crotch lower line by selecting the bottom line with the *Direct Selection Tool*.

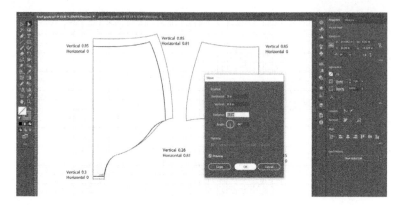

6. Repeat the grade on the front pattern piece as demonstrated above. Repeat all steps for each size in the graded size set.

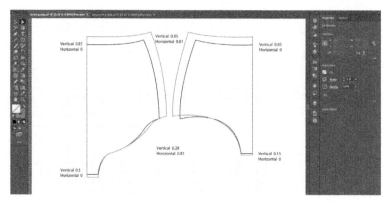

PATTERNS

CHAPTER 21

PATTERN INSTRUCTIONS

To determine the best size, review the size charts below and select the most appropriate size. This book contains sizes XS through XL. These patterns are also available for download on our website at porcelynne.com, as an option under the book.

The patterns included with this book are designed for a knit fabric with a 50% stretch in the width and a 35% stretch in the length.

IMPERIAL SIZE CHART

Measurements in Inches

Letter Sizes	XS	S	M	L	XL
US Number Sizes	0-2	4-6	8-10	12-14	16-18
UK Number Sizes	4-6	8-10	12-14	16-18	20-22
Waist Measurement	22-25	26-29	30-33	34-37	38-41
Hip Measurement	32-35	36-39	40-43	44-47	48-51

METRIC SIZE CHART

Measurements in Centimeters

Letter Sizes	XS	S	M	L	XL
US Number Sizes	0-2	4-6	8-10	12-14	16-18
UK Number Sizes	4-6	8-10	12-14	16-18	20-22
EU Number Sizes	32-34	36-38	40-42	44-46	48-50
Italy Number Sizes	36-38	40-42	44-46	48-50	52-54
Japan Number Sizes	3-5	7-9	11-13	15-17	19-21
Australia Number Sizes	6-8	10-12	14-16	18-20	22-24
Waist Measurement	56-65	66-75	76-85	86-96	97-107
Hip Measurement	81-90	91-101	102-111	112-121	122-131

BOYSHORT PATTERN

Extra Large

Large

Medium

Small

Extra Small

1" Square

1 cm

Bare Essentials
Basic Boyshort
Back
Sizes XS-XL
Cut 2
1/4" or 6 mm Seam Allowance
www.Porcelynne.com

1" Square

1 cm

1" Square

1 cm

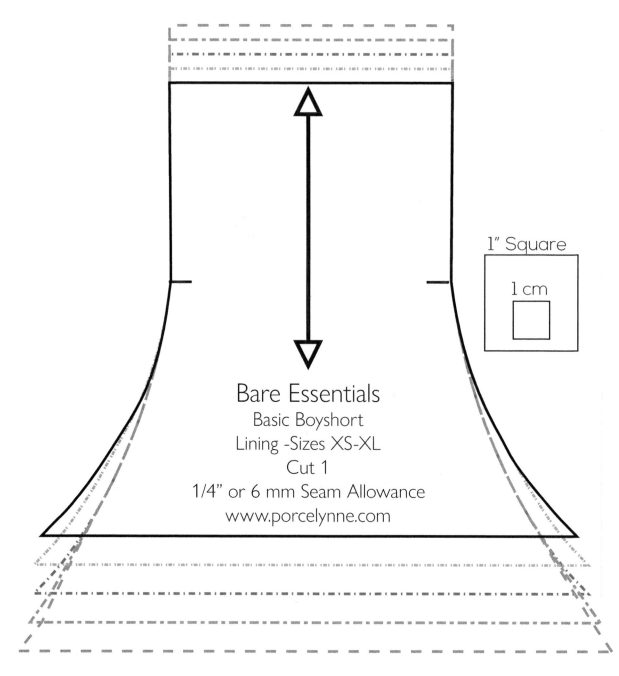

Bare Essentials
Basic Boyshort
Lining -Sizes XS-XL
Cut 1
1/4" or 6 mm Seam Allowance
www.porcelynne.com

1" Square

1 cm

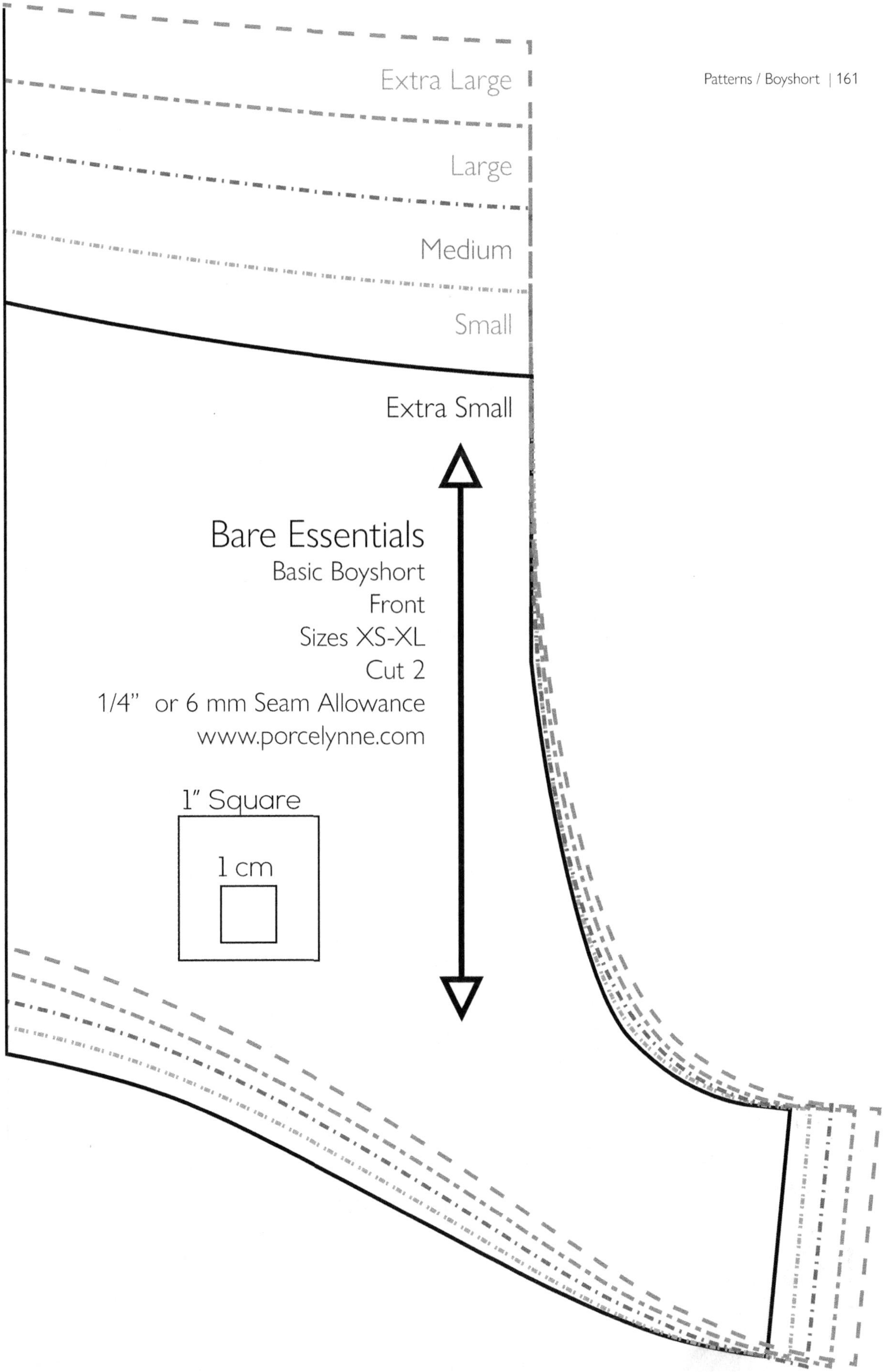

Extra Large

Large

Medium

Small

Extra Small

Bare Essentials
Basic Boyshort
Front
Sizes XS-XL
Cut 2
1/4" or 6 mm Seam Allowance
www.porcelynne.com

1" Square

1 cm

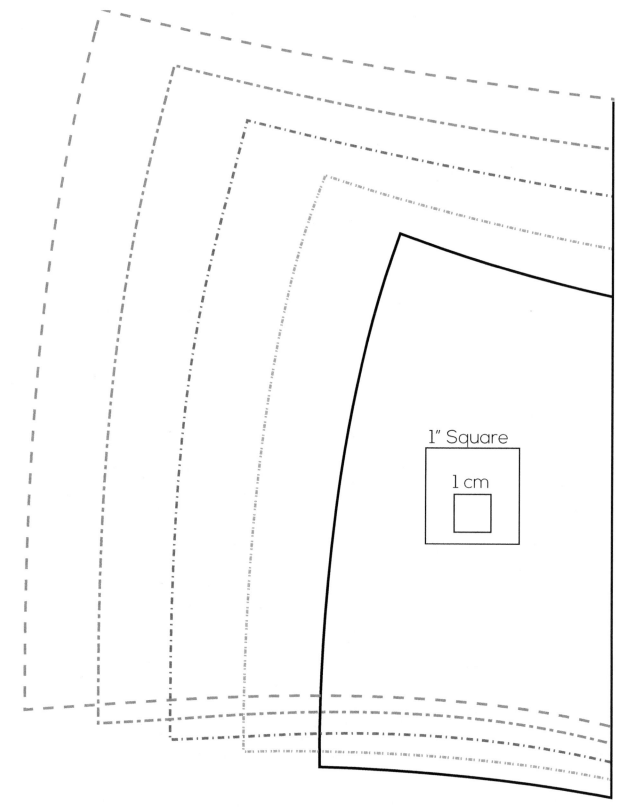

1" Square

1 cm

BRIEF PATTERN

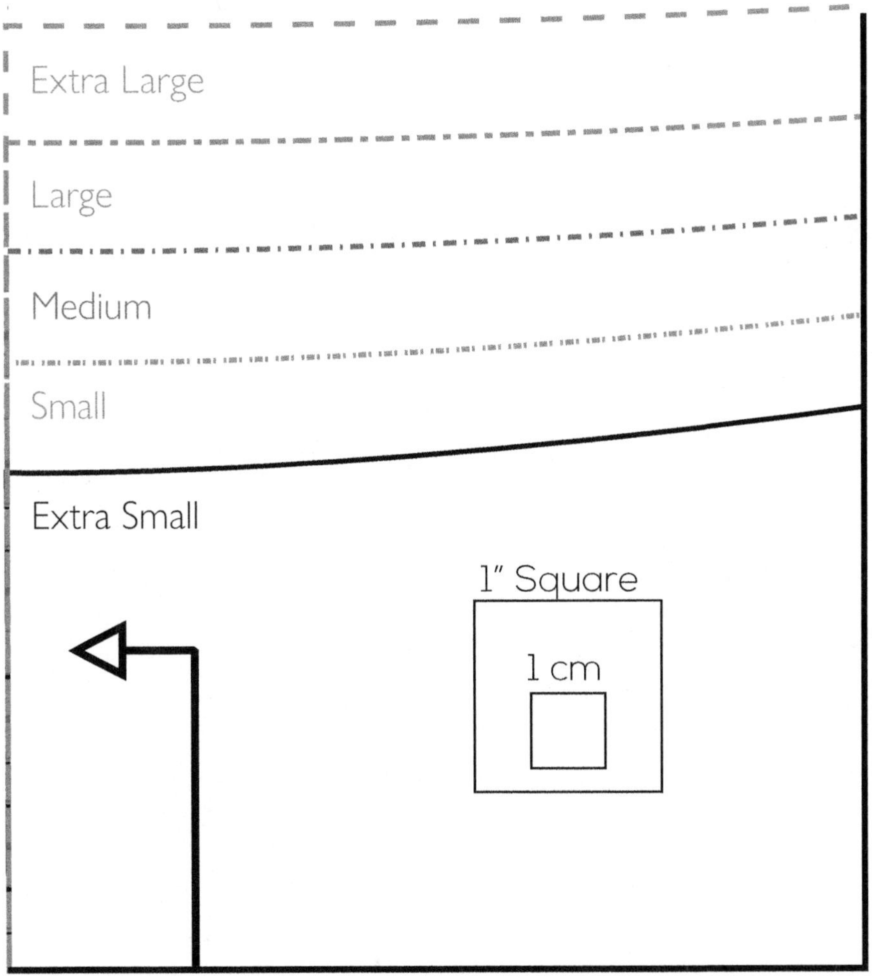

Extra Large

Large

Medium

Small

Extra Small

1" Square

1 cm

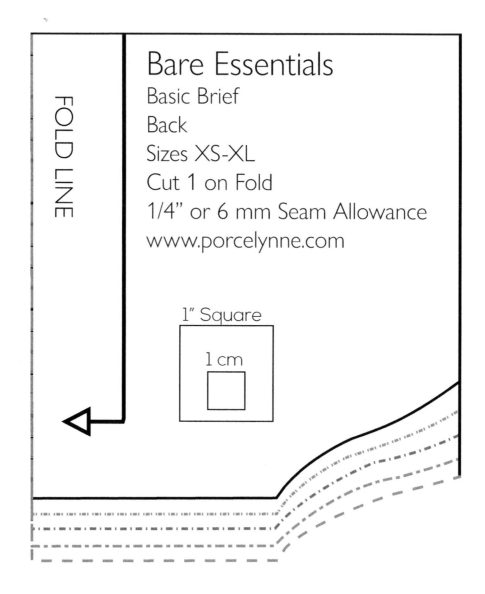

FOLD LINE

Bare Essentials
Basic Brief
Back
Sizes XS-XL
Cut 1 on Fold
1/4" or 6 mm Seam Allowance
www.porcelynne.com

1" Square

1 cm

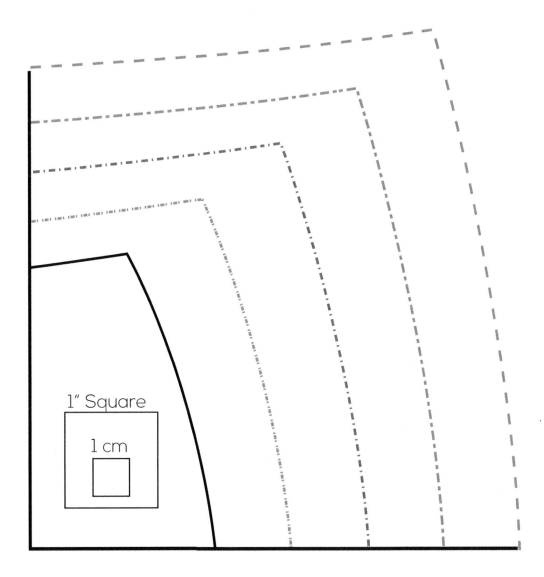

1" Square

1 cm

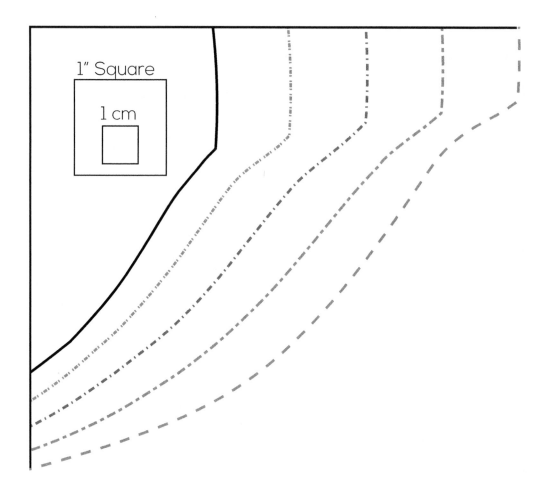

1" Square

1 cm

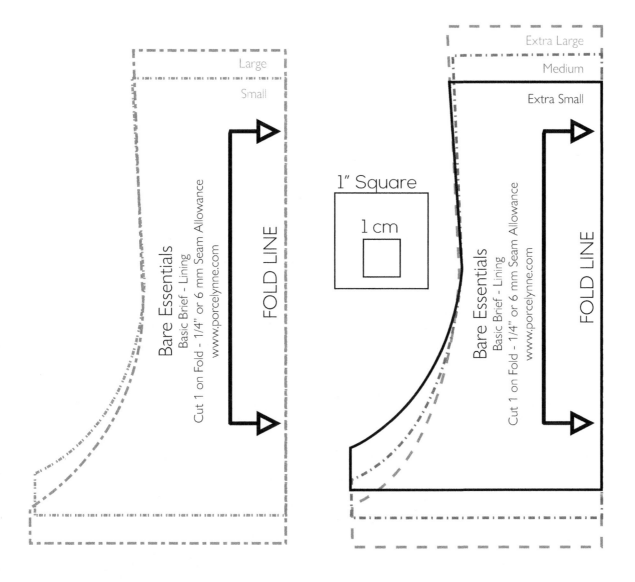

Large
Small

Bare Essentials
Basic Brief - Lining
Cut 1 on Fold - 1/4" or 6 mm Seam Allowance
www.porcelynne.com

FOLD LINE

1" Square

1 cm

Extra Large
Medium
Extra Small

Bare Essentials
Basic Brief - Lining
Cut 1 on Fold - 1/4" or 6 mm Seam Allowance
www.porcelynne.com

FOLD LINE

1" Square

1 cm

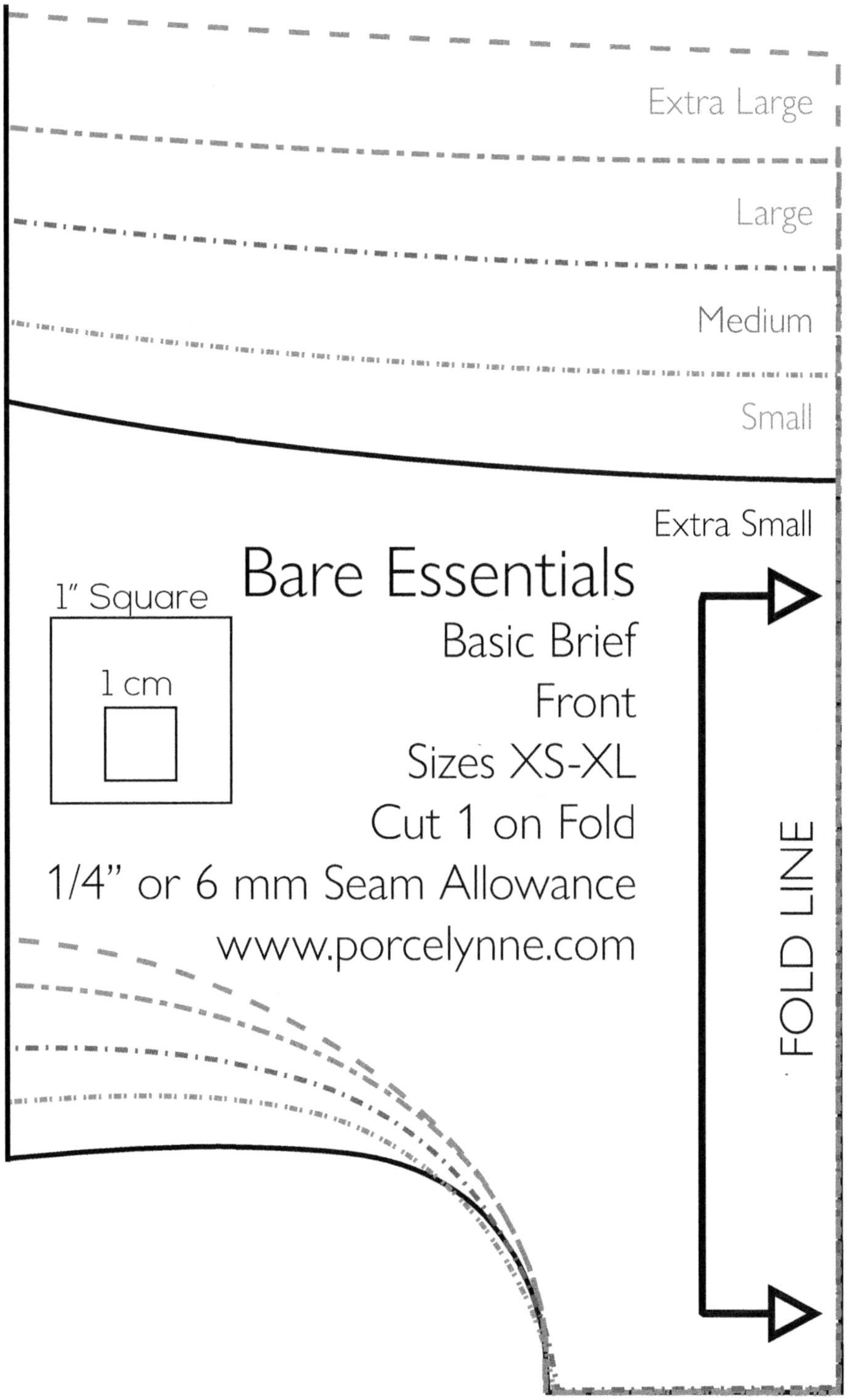

Extra Large

Large

Medium

Small

Extra Small

1" Square

1 cm

Bare Essentials
Basic Brief
Front
Sizes XS-XL
Cut 1 on Fold
1/4" or 6 mm Seam Allowance
www.porcelynne.com

FOLD LINE

Printed in Great Britain
by Amazon

84131924R00099